The AI-Powered Classroom

A Teacher's Step-by-Step Guide to Using AI in Education

Patty R. Adams

Table of Contents

Thank You for Reading!

I hope you found *The AI-Powered Classroom*
A Teacher's Step-by-Step Guide to Using AI in
Education helpful and enjoyable!
Your feedback is invaluable to me and helps others discover
this book.

If you could take a moment to **leave a review**, I'd
greatly appreciate it.   Scan the QR code below to
leave your review:

Thank you,

Patty R. Adams

Introduction

The first time I witnessed AI's true potential in my classroom wasn't during a perfectly executed lesson or a breakthrough technology moment. It was on a Tuesday afternoon when Jamie, one of my struggling writers, finally found his voice.

For months, I had watched this bright but anxious student agonize over every writing assignment, his fear of failure paralyzing his creativity. Then, using an AI writing assistant as a brainstorming partner, Jamie began to transform. The technology didn't write for him; instead, it helped him explore ideas, organize his thoughts, and build confidence in his own abilities. By the end of the semester, Jamie wasn't just writing; he was thriving.

This book was born from moments like these; moments when I realized that AI isn't here to replace the magic that happens in our classrooms. It's here to amplify it. To help us do what we've always done best: inspire, guide, and empower our students to become confident, capable learners.

But let's be honest. If you're picking up this book, you probably have mixed feelings about AI in education. Maybe you've watched with growing concern as AI tools have transformed how students approach writing and research. Perhaps you've experienced that sinking feeling when you suspect an essay isn't entirely student-generated, or you've struggled to redesign assignments that suddenly feel vulnerable to AI manipulation.

You might be wondering: How do I maintain academic integrity in an AI-powered world? Can I really use these tools without compromising my teaching values? Will AI make my students better thinkers or just better cheaters?

These are the questions that kept me up at night, too. As a veteran teacher with over fifteen years in the classroom, I've weathered my share of technological transformations. But AI felt different; more fundamental, more challenging, and yes, more frightening.

This book is your practical guide to navigating this transformation. Whether you're AI-curious but cautious, or you're already experimenting with these tools but seeking more structured approaches, you'll find strategies you can implement immediately and frameworks you can adapt to your unique classroom needs.

In the following chapters, we'll explore how to:

- Use AI as a time-saving teaching assistant while maintaining your professional judgment and personal touch
- Design assignments that harness AI's potential while protecting academic integrity
- Build students' critical thinking skills in an AI-enhanced learning environment
- Create sustainable, ethical approaches to AI integration across your curriculum

Most importantly, we'll focus on practical solutions that work in real classrooms, with real students, and real-world constraints. No theoretical frameworks that fall apart on Monday morning. No tech-heavy solutions that require a computer science degree. Just straightforward strategies that help you work smarter, not harder.

Remember Jamie? His story isn't unique. Every day, teachers across the country are discovering how to use AI tools to unlock student potential, save precious time, and enhance rather than diminish the human elements of teaching. This book will show you how to become one of them.

So take a deep breath. You've got this. And I'm here to help you every step of the way.

Let's begin.

Chapter 1:

The AI-Empowered Teacher: Understanding Your New Digital Assistant

The first time I asked an AI to help me create a lesson plan, my hands were actually shaking; I felt like I was somehow cheating at my job. Looking back now, I realize that moment wasn't about betraying my teaching principles; it was about discovering a powerful tool that would transform how I prepare, teach, and support my students. Those first weeks of experimenting with AI in my classroom were a rollercoaster of emotions; excitement mixed with uncertainty, hope tinged with hesitation. Like many teachers, I worried that embracing AI tools might somehow diminish the craft I'd spent years perfecting. But what I discovered instead was a partnership that enhanced rather than replaced my teaching expertise.

Let me share a story that might feel familiar. Hope Martinez, a veteran English teacher with twelve years of experience, found herself facing an impossible stack of 150 essays that needed feedback by Friday. We've all been there: that mounting pressure of deadlines coupled with our deep desire to give each student meaningful feedback. Hope's journey from AI skeptic to confident user mirrors what many of us experience as we navigate this new educational landscape.

Hope's story resonates because it captures a critical truth about AI in education: this technology isn't here to replace our expertise or diminish the human elements of teaching. Instead, it's a tool that, when used thoughtfully, can amplify our effectiveness and free us to focus on what matters most: meaningful interactions with our students.

In this chapter, we'll explore the foundations of the teacher-AI partnership and address the questions that keep many of us up at night: How can AI truly help without compromising educational quality? What are the practical first steps? How do we maintain our professional judgment while leveraging these new tools? Through real classroom examples and practical strategies, we'll build a framework for understanding and using AI that honors both technological innovation and pedagogical wisdom.

As we begin this journey together, remember that becoming AI-empowered doesn't mean becoming less human in our teaching. In fact, it's quite the opposite. When we harness AI effectively, we create more space for the deeply human aspects of education - the moments of connection, revelation, and growth that drew us to teaching in the first place.

Let's start by examining three fundamental aspects of the teacher-AI partnership:

- Understanding AI's role as an assistant, not a replacement
- Setting clear boundaries for ethical AI use in education
- Identifying opportunities for AI to enhance rather than diminish our teaching practice

Through Hope's story, we saw how AI tools could transform a daunting grading task into a manageable process while actually improving feedback quality. Her experience highlights a crucial point: AI implementation works best when it begins with a specific challenge and focuses on practical solutions. Over the next few months, Hope developed a systematic approach that cut her grading time in half while maintaining, and often improving, the quality of her student feedback. She found herself with more energy to innovate in other areas of her teaching, proving that technology, when properly harnessed, can help us become better versions of ourselves as educators.

This transformation didn't happen overnight, and it wasn't without its challenges. But by taking small, intentional steps and maintaining focus on student learning outcomes, Hope discovered a balanced approach to AI integration that worked for her classroom. Her journey from hesitation to confident implementation serves as a roadmap for our own exploration of AI in education.

As we delve deeper into the practical applications of AI in teaching, remember that this isn't about completely overhauling your teaching style or adopting every available tool. Instead, it's about thoughtfully selecting and implementing AI solutions that align with your pedagogical goals and enhance your existing teaching practices. The key is starting small, focusing on specific challenges, and gradually building confidence with these new tools.

Demystifying AI: Understanding the Basics of Your Digital Teaching Assistant

Let's start with a confession: when someone first explained AI to me using terms like "machine learning algorithms" and "neural networks," my eyes glazed over faster than a student's during a grammar lesson. But here's what I've learned: understanding AI doesn't require a computer science degree. It just needs a shift in how we think about these tools.

At its core, AI is like having a very eager teaching assistant who's incredibly fast at processing information but needs clear instructions and careful oversight. Think of it as a powerful pattern-recognition tool that's been trained on vast amounts of data, from texts and lesson plans to student writing samples and educational resources.[3] It can analyze this information and generate new content based on what it's learned, much like how we might draw on our years of teaching experience to create new lessons or provide feedback.

But here's what makes AI different from traditional technology: it can adapt and learn from interactions.[2, 3] When we use AI tools like language models or adaptive learning platforms, they're not just following pre-programmed rules; they're actually adjusting their responses based on the input they receive. This is why AI can feel almost human-like in its interactions, while still being fundamentally different from human intelligence.

Let's break down the key types of AI tools you're likely to encounter in education:

- Generative AI: These tools can create text, answer questions, and help with tasks like lesson planning and feedback generation[4]
- Adaptive Learning Systems: Platforms that adjust to individual student needs and progress[1, 2]
- Automation Tools: Programs that help streamline grading, scheduling, and administrative tasks[1, 2]

Understanding these distinctions helps us make better decisions about when and how to use AI in our classrooms. For instance, generative AI might be perfect for brainstorming discussion questions, but you'll want to carefully review and modify its suggestions based on your knowledge of your specific students and curriculum.

One crucial aspect of working with AI is understanding its limitations. These tools are incredibly powerful, but they're not infallible. They can make mistakes, show biases (based on their training data), and sometimes generate plausible-sounding but incorrect information.[1, 4] This is why teacher oversight remains essential; we bring the professional judgment, ethical awareness, and deep understanding of our students that AI simply cannot replicate.

Here's a practical way to think about AI's role in your classroom: it's not about replacing your expertise but about amplifying it.[1, 2] When used thoughtfully, AI can handle many time-consuming tasks, allowing you to focus on the aspects of teaching that require human insight and connection. For example, while AI might help generate initial feedback on student essays, you can use the time saved to have meaningful one-on-one conferences with students about their writing progress.

Developing AI literacy - the ability to understand, evaluate, and effectively use AI tools - is becoming as essential for educators as basic digital literacy was a decade ago.[1, 2, 3] This doesn't mean becoming a tech expert, but rather developing a working knowledge of:

- When AI tools can be helpful (and when they might not be)
- How to evaluate AI-generated content for accuracy and appropriateness[1, 3]
- Ways to model ethical AI use for your students[1, 2]

As we move forward in this chapter, we'll explore practical strategies for integrating AI into your teaching practice, always keeping in mind that you're in charge; AI is your assistant, not your replacement.[1, 2] Remember, the goal isn't to become an AI expert but to become confident enough to use these tools effectively while maintaining your professional judgment and teaching integrity.

The key to success with AI is starting small and focusing on specific challenges in your teaching practice.[2, 3] Maybe you begin by using AI to help generate differentiated writing prompts, or perhaps you explore how it can help create more engaging lesson hooks. Whatever your starting point, remember that this is a journey of experimentation and growth, and you don't have to figure it all out at once.

In the next section, we'll look at specific strategies for setting realistic expectations and boundaries with AI tools, ensuring that they enhance rather than complicate your teaching practice. But for now, take a deep breath and remember: you've got this. After all, adapting to new tools while keeping student learning at the center is what great teachers do best.

The Teacher-AI Partnership: Setting Realistic Expectations and Boundaries

When I first started using AI in my classroom, I treated it like that enthusiastic but sometimes overeager student teacher; you know the one. They're full of great ideas but need clear boundaries and guidance to be truly effective.[1, 2, 3] This analogy has helped countless teachers I've worked with understand how to approach their own AI partnerships.

Let's be clear about what AI can and cannot do in our classrooms. AI excels at processing information, recognizing patterns, and automating routine tasks.[1, 2] It can help us grade multiple-choice assessments, generate initial feedback on essays, or create differentiated practice exercises.[1, 2, 5] But it lacks human intuition, emotional intelligence, and the ability to truly understand our students' unique contexts and needs.[1, 2, 3]

Here are the key boundaries we need to establish when working with AI:

- AI assists but doesn't replace teacher judgment[1, 2, 5]
- Student data privacy must be protected at all times[1, 2, 3]
- Academic integrity remains paramount[3]
- Equity and accessibility guide all AI implementation[1, 2]
- Human connection stays at the heart of teaching[1, 3]

Think of AI as your digital teaching assistant; one that can handle routine tasks while you focus on what matters most: building relationships with students, providing nuanced feedback, and creating meaningful learning experiences.[1,2,5] For instance, while AI can help generate initial writing prompts or rubric criteria, you'll always need to review and adjust these based on your knowledge of your students' needs and abilities.[3]

One crucial aspect of setting realistic expectations is understanding that not everything should be automated. Some of our most important work as educators, motivating students, providing emotional support, and fostering creativity, requires human insight and connection.[1,3] The goal isn't to delegate these critical functions to AI but to use it strategically to create more time for these essential human interactions.[1,2,3]

When it comes to protecting student privacy and maintaining academic integrity, we need clear guidelines. Always vet AI tools for compliance with privacy regulations and be transparent with students and parents about how these tools handle personal information.[1,2,3] In terms of assessment, design assignments that prioritize human effort and creativity, making it more difficult to outsource work entirely to AI.[2,3]

Here are practical strategies for maintaining healthy boundaries with AI:

- Regularly review and adjust which tasks you delegate to AI[3]
- Keep a human eye on AI-generated content and feedback[3]

- Ensure equitable access to AI tools across your student population[1, 2]
- Model ethical AI use for your students[1, 2]
- Maintain open dialogue about AI's role in your classroom[2, 3]

Developing AI literacy is becoming as essential as basic digital literacy was a decade ago.[1, 2, 3] This doesn't mean becoming a tech expert; it means understanding enough about AI's capabilities and limitations to use it effectively while maintaining your professional judgment and teaching integrity.[1, 2]

Remember, you're in charge of this partnership. Just as you would guide a student teacher, you need to direct AI's efforts, review its work, and ensure it aligns with your teaching goals and values.[1, 2, 3] When used thoughtfully, AI can enhance rather than diminish your role as an educator.[1, 5, 3]

As we navigate this partnership, it's crucial to stay reflective about how AI impacts teaching quality, student engagement, and learning outcomes.[2] Regular self-assessment and student feedback can help ensure we're using AI in ways that truly benefit our educational mission.[2, 3]

The key is finding the right balance; using AI to handle routine tasks while preserving the irreplaceable human elements of teaching.[1, 2, 5] Start small, perhaps with one specific task like generating differentiated vocabulary exercises or creating initial feedback templates.[1, 5] As you become more comfortable, you can gradually expand your AI collaboration while maintaining clear boundaries and high standards for student learning.[2, 3]

Remember, you're not alone in this journey. Teachers across the country are working to find this balance, sharing successes and learning from challenges.[2, 5] By establishing clear boundaries and realistic expectations from the start, we can create AI partnerships that enhance our teaching while protecting what makes education truly meaningful: the human connection at its heart.[1, 2, 3]

Getting Started: Essential AI Tools for the Modern Classroom

When I first ventured into using AI tools in my classroom, I felt like I was standing in the educational technology aisle of a mega-store, overwhelmed by choices and unsure where to begin. If you're feeling the same way, take a deep breath. We're going to break this down into manageable pieces, focusing on the essential tools that can make a real difference in your teaching practice without overwhelming you or your students.[8, 9]

Let's start with a fundamental truth: the best AI tools for education are those that solve real classroom challenges while remaining intuitive enough that you can implement them without a computer science degree.[7, 6] The key is to begin with tools that integrate seamlessly into platforms you're already using.

One standout example is Google's Notebook LM, which has become a favorite among educators for its ability to analyze and synthesize information from various sources into student-friendly resources.[7, 8] Think of it as your digital teaching assistant that can help create study guides, timelines, and briefing documents; all while working within the familiar Google Classroom environment you likely already use.[8]

Here are the essential AI tools that every modern classroom should consider:

- Content Creation and Summarization Tools (like Notebook LM and Gemini in the Classroom)
- Language and Communication Enhancement Platforms
- Personalized Learning and Differentiation Systems
- Time-Saving Administrative Tools
- Collaboration and Professional Learning Networks

Let's be practical about implementation. Start with one tool that addresses your most pressing need. For instance, if you're spending hours creating differentiated content, Gemini in Classroom offers over 30 no-cost AI features specifically designed for this purpose.[8] It can help you generate various versions of the same material for different learning levels, all while maintaining the core learning objectives.

One of the most exciting developments is the integration of AI speech recognition tools in language instruction. These tools can provide real-time pronunciation feedback and create adaptive learning pathways, freeing you to focus on the more nuanced aspects of language teaching.[6] The technology isn't replacing your expertise; it's amplifying it.

When it comes to assessment and grading, AI tools can be game-changers for time management. Automated grading systems can handle objective assessments while providing instant feedback to students.[9] However, remember that these tools should complement, not replace, your professional judgment. Use them for initial feedback or routine tasks, saving your expertise for more complex evaluations.

Here's a practical tip for getting started: identify your most time-consuming task. Is it grading multiple-choice assessments? Creating differentiated worksheets? Providing basic writing feedback? Choose one AI tool that addresses that specific challenge and master it before moving on to others.[9] This focused approach prevents overwhelm and helps you build confidence with AI integration.

Data security and student privacy should always be at the forefront of your AI implementation strategy. Before adopting any new tool, ensure it complies with your school's privacy requirements and data protection standards. Many educators find success starting with tools that are already embedded in approved platforms like Google Classroom,[8] as these have typically been vetted for educational use.

The professional learning aspect of AI integration shouldn't be overlooked either. Platforms like Blue Sky are emerging as valuable resources for educators to connect, share experiences, and learn from each other's AI implementation journeys.[7] Remember, you're not alone in this process; there's a growing community of educators navigating these same waters.

As you begin incorporating these tools, keep in mind that the goal isn't to automate everything; it's to enhance your teaching while preserving what makes education meaningful: the human connection.[6] Start small, focus on tools that solve real problems in your classroom, and give yourself permission to learn and adjust as you go.

Remember, the best AI implementation strategy is one that you can sustain and that genuinely serves your students' needs. You don't need to transform your entire teaching practice overnight. Begin with one tool, master it, and then expand your AI toolkit as your confidence grows. The modern classroom isn't about having every possible AI tool; it's about thoughtfully selecting and implementing the ones that truly enhance learning and save you time.[9]

In the next section, we'll dive deeper into specific strategies for using these tools effectively while maintaining academic integrity and promoting student engagement. But for now, focus on exploring one or two tools that align with your immediate needs. You've got this, and remember, every expert was once a beginner. As we conclude this first chapter, let's take a moment to reflect on our journey from AI anxiety to AI empowerment. We began with Hope Martinez staring down that intimidating stack of essays, feeling overwhelmed but willing to try something new. Her story mirrors the path many of us are on: moving from hesitation to strategic implementation, from fear to focused purpose.

Through our exploration of AI basics, boundary-setting, and essential tools, we've established some fundamental truths about teaching in the AI age:

- AI is a powerful assistant, not a replacement for your expertise
- Clear boundaries and ethical guidelines are essential for successful implementation
- Starting small and focusing on specific challenges leads to sustainable integration

- The goal is to enhance, not diminish, the human elements of teaching

Remember that Tuesday evening when I first sat down to use AI tools, hands shaking as I typed in that first prompt? Looking back now, I realize that moment wasn't just about learning to use a new tool; it was about reimagining what's possible in our classrooms while staying true to our values as educators.

As we move forward into more specific applications in the coming chapters, keep in mind that this journey isn't about becoming an AI expert overnight. It's about thoughtfully selecting and implementing tools that align with your teaching goals and enhance your existing practices. You don't need to transform your entire teaching approach at once; start with one challenge, one tool, one solution at a time.

Before we dive into AI tools in Chapter 2, take a moment to identify one specific teaching task you'd like to enhance with AI assistance. Perhaps it's generating differentiated writing prompts, creating initial feedback templates, or streamlining lesson planning. Whatever you choose, remember that you're not alone on this journey; thousands of teachers are taking these same first steps alongside you.

The path to becoming an AI-empowered teacher isn't about racing to adopt every new tool or completely overhauling your teaching style. It's about thoughtfully integrating technology in ways that preserve what makes teaching meaningful while reducing the administrative burden that can lead to burnout. As we've seen through Hope's story and our exploration of AI fundamentals, the key is starting small, staying focused on student needs, and maintaining your professional judgment throughout the process.

You've already taken the first and most important step: choosing to engage with AI intentionally and ethically. In the chapters ahead, we'll build on this foundation, exploring specific strategies for writing instruction, research skills, and assessment. But for now, celebrate this beginning. You're not just adapting to new technology; you're helping shape the future of education.

Remember: You've got this. Your experience, your insight, and your dedication to student success are irreplaceable. AI is just a tool; you're the teacher who will transform it into something meaningful for your students.

Chapter 2:

Classroom AI Tools: Your Essential Teaching Tech Stack

The modern classroom isn't just about smart boards and tablets anymore; it's about knowing which AI tools can truly transform your teaching without overwhelming you or your students. As we dive into building your essential AI teaching toolkit, remember that the goal isn't to adopt every shiny new tool, but to carefully select and master the ones that will make the biggest impact in your specific classroom context. As we explore the essential tools that will shape your AI-enhanced classroom, let's start with a story that might feel familiar. Blake Thompson, a veteran teacher known for his meticulous organization, found himself drowning in a sea of new AI platforms mid-semester. His desk was littered with sticky notes bearing different login credentials, and his teaching time was increasingly consumed by technology troubleshooting rather than actual instruction.

But Blake's journey from overwhelmed to empowered offers us valuable insights about building an effective AI toolkit. Through systematic evaluation and thoughtful implementation, he discovered that success wasn't about adopting every available tool; it was about finding the right ones that genuinely enhanced his teaching practice and students' learning experience.

In this chapter, we'll explore how to build your own streamlined AI toolkit, focusing on tools that integrate seamlessly with your existing teaching methods while genuinely saving you time and enhancing student learning. We'll examine practical frameworks for evaluating AI tools, explore essential applications for content creation and assessment, and develop sustainable workflows that work in real classroom settings.

Like Blake, you'll learn to move beyond the initial overwhelm and develop a focused approach to selecting and implementing AI tools. We'll look at specific strategies for content creation, assessment, and student engagement that can transform your teaching without requiring you to become a tech expert. The goal isn't to revolutionize everything you're doing; it's to enhance your existing practices with tools that actually make sense for your classroom.

As we dive deeper into specific tools and applications, remember that this isn't about completely overhauling your teaching style or abandoning tried-and-true methods. Instead, think of it as adding new instruments to your teaching orchestra; each tool should harmonize with your existing practice while expanding your capabilities to reach and engage students more effectively.

By the end of this chapter, you'll have a clear framework for evaluating and selecting AI tools, understanding which ones deserve a place in your teaching toolkit, and implementing them in ways that enhance rather than complicate your teaching practice. Let's begin building your essential AI teaching toolkit; one that works for you, not the other way around.

Selecting and Evaluating Educational AI Tools: A Teacher's Framework

When it comes to choosing AI tools for your classroom, it's easy to feel like you're standing in front of an endless buffet without knowing what's actually good for you. With new educational AI tools launching seemingly every week, we need a practical way to separate the truly helpful from the merely flashy.[2, 3, 10] Let's build a framework that helps you make confident choices about which AI tools deserve a place in your teaching toolkit.

First, let's acknowledge what matters most: any AI tool we bring into our classroom should genuinely enhance learning while respecting student privacy and promoting academic integrity.[3, 11] Think of this framework as your trusted checklist; one that prioritizes both practical value and ethical considerations.

Start with these essential questions:

- Does this tool align with my specific teaching goals?[10]
- How will it directly benefit my students' learning?[2, 10]
- Is it secure and protective of student privacy?[11]
- Can all my students access and use it effectively?[10]
- Does it save me time without compromising quality?[2, 10]

Let's break this down into actionable steps. When evaluating any AI tool, begin by defining the specific instructional need or problem you're trying to solve.[2, 3, 10, 11] Are you looking to streamline feedback on student writing? Generate differentiated reading assignments?

Create more engaging discussion prompts? Being clear about your purpose helps narrow the field immediately.

Next, investigate the tool's privacy and security features. This isn't just about being cautious; it's about protecting our students. Look for tools that are transparent about their data practices and comply with educational privacy standards.[11] If a tool's privacy policy reads like a mystery novel, that's a red flag.

Usability is another crucial factor. The best AI tool in the world won't help if it takes hours to learn or frequently crashes during class. Look for tools with intuitive interfaces and reliable performance.[10] Better yet, seek out tools that integrate with platforms you're already using, like Google Classroom or your school's learning management system.

Consider equity and accessibility. Will all your students be able to use this tool effectively? Does it offer features for English language learners or students with learning differences?[10, 11] The goal is to close achievement gaps, not widen them.

Here's a practical way to test drive a new AI tool:

- Try it yourself first with a small, low-stakes task
- Pilot it with a single class or small group of students
- Gather feedback about what works and what doesn't
- Monitor the impact on both teaching and learning
- Document your findings to inform future decisions[2, 3, 10, 11]

Remember, you don't need to implement every promising tool at once. Start with one that addresses your most pressing need, master it, and then consider adding others.[10] This measured approach helps prevent technology overload while ensuring you're using each tool effectively.

When evaluating AI tools, also consider the level of support available. Are there clear tutorials or help resources? Is there an active community of educators using the tool who can share insights and troubleshooting tips?[10] These support systems can make the difference between successful implementation and frustrated abandonment.

Finally, don't forget to assess the cost-benefit ratio. While some excellent AI tools are free, others require subscriptions or licenses.[10] Consider not just the monetary cost, but also the time investment required to implement the tool effectively. Sometimes, a paid tool that saves hours of work each week is worth the investment, while a free tool that requires constant troubleshooting might not be worth the hassle.

As you apply this framework, trust your professional judgment. You know your students, your teaching style, and your classroom needs better than any AI company's marketing team.[2, 10] Use these guidelines as a starting point, but let your expertise and experience guide your final decisions.

Remember, the goal isn't to use AI for everything; it's to use it strategically where it can truly enhance teaching and learning while maintaining the human elements that make education meaningful.[2, 3] By applying this framework thoughtfully, you can build an AI toolkit that serves you and your students effectively while upholding the values that matter most in education.

Core AI Tools for Content Creation and Assessment

Let's dive into the essential AI tools that can transform how we create and assess student work, without turning our classrooms into tech laboratories. Think of these tools as your digital teaching assistants, ready to help with everything from lesson planning to assessment creation, while keeping the focus on what matters most: authentic learning and student growth.

First up in our AI toolkit are content creation powerhouses that can help us develop engaging materials more efficiently. Curipod, for instance, has become a go-to resource for many teachers looking to quickly generate interactive lessons. With just a topic input, it creates ready-to-use content complete with text, images, and interactive elements like polls and word clouds.[12] It's particularly helpful when you need to put together a last-minute lesson plan or want to add some variety to your existing materials.

Eduaide.AI offers another comprehensive solution, especially valuable for teachers working with diverse learners. With features like instant translation into more than 15 languages and tools for creating individualized education program (IEP) materials, it helps ensure our content reaches every student.[12] The platform's assessment builder has been a game-changer for many educators, allowing them to quickly generate differentiated assessments while maintaining high standards.

When it comes to assessment tools, we're seeing some exciting developments that help us save time without compromising quality.

The assessment features in platforms like Eduaide.AI and Learnt.AI allow us to generate various question types, from multiple-choice to open-ended responses, all aligned with our learning objectives.[12, 13] These tools aren't replacing our expertise; they're amplifying it, helping us create more comprehensive and varied assessments in less time.

However, it's crucial to remember that these tools are meant to enhance, not replace, our professional judgment. According to Google's research on AI in education, 83% of educators report saving over two hours weekly using generative AI tools.[14] But the key is using them strategically and ethically.

Here are some practical guidelines for integrating these tools effectively:

- Always review AI-generated content for accuracy and appropriateness before using it with students[12]
- Use AI tools to create initial drafts or templates, then customize them for your specific classroom needs
- Maintain a balance between AI-assisted and traditional assessment methods
- Prioritize tools that integrate well with your existing classroom technology
- Consider privacy and data security when selecting new tools

One particularly powerful way to use these tools is for differentiation. For example, you might use Eduaide.AI to quickly create multiple versions of the same assignment at different reading levels, or generate varied practice questions for students who need extra support.[12] This kind of customization used to take hours; now it can be done in minutes.

When it comes to assessment, these tools really shine in formative evaluation. They can help us quickly generate exit tickets, create practice questions, or develop rubrics.[12, 13] But remember, the goal isn't to automate assessment entirely. Instead, use these tools to handle the time-consuming aspects of assessment creation so you can focus more energy on providing meaningful feedback and supporting student growth.

Let's talk about workflow integration, because that's where many teachers initially struggle. Start small; choose one tool and one specific task, like using Curipod for warm-up activities or Learnt.AI for generating discussion prompts.[12, 13] Once you're comfortable with that, gradually expand your AI toolkit based on your needs and comfort level.

Remember, you don't need to master every AI tool available. The key is finding the right combination of tools that work for your teaching style and your students' needs. As Google's education research emphasizes, AI should support, not replace, teacher expertise and creativity.[15]

Before implementing any new AI tool, ask yourself these essential questions:

- Will this tool genuinely save me time once I learn to use it effectively?

- Does it align with my teaching goals and philosophy?
- Can all my students access and benefit from this tool?
- Does it maintain high standards for academic integrity?
- Is it secure and protective of student privacy?

By thoughtfully selecting and implementing these AI tools, we can create more engaging content and meaningful assessments while actually reducing our workload. The goal isn't to revolutionize everything we're doing; it's to enhance our existing practices with tools that make sense for our classrooms.

As we continue to explore these tools, remember that you're not alone in this journey. Many of your colleagues are navigating the same waters, and the evidence shows that teachers who thoughtfully integrate AI tools are finding more time for what matters most: meaningful interactions with their students.[14]

Building Effective AI Workflows: From Planning to Feedback

Creating an effective AI workflow in your classroom doesn't have to feel like juggling chainsaws while riding a unicycle. Let's break down how to build sustainable, ethical processes that actually make your life easier, not more complicated. After all, the goal is to enhance your teaching, not add another layer of tech stress to your already full plate.

Let's start with a fundamental truth: AI literacy is essential for both educators and students in today's classroom.[1, 2, 3] As J.A. Bowen reminds us, helping every student experience "I care, I can, I matter" in an age of AI may be the most important lesson we can teach.[3] This means understanding not just how to use AI tools, but when and why they're appropriate.

Here's a practical framework for building your AI workflow:

- Start with clear educational objectives; what specific teaching goals are you trying to achieve?[2, 3, 4]
- Choose AI tools that align with these goals and integrate smoothly with your existing practices[2]
- Establish clear AI use policies for your classroom[3, 4]
- Build in regular checkpoints for reviewing and adjusting your approach

When it comes to planning, think of AI as your collaborative partner, not a replacement for your expertise.[1, 2, 3] Use it to automate routine tasks like generating initial lesson ideas or creating basic rubric templates[1, 2, 3] This frees up your time and mental energy for the aspects of teaching that truly require human insight; like understanding your students' unique needs and providing nuanced feedback.

Implementation is where many teachers initially stumble, but here's the secret: start small. Choose one routine task that takes up too much of your time; maybe it's creating differentiated writing prompts or providing basic feedback on drafts. Use AI to help with this specific task until it becomes natural, then gradually expand your AI toolkit as your confidence grows.

For daily classroom practice, consider using AI for:

- Generating quick formative assessments
- Differentiating instruction for diverse learners[1, 2]
- Creating scaffolded learning materials
- Providing instant, basic feedback on student work[3, 4]

However, remember what Aaron Blackwelder and Jason Cowley emphasize: "AI will not diminish the need for students to learn essential skills. It will, however, change how we teach and will require us to develop new skill sets for instruction and assessment."[2]

When it comes to feedback and assessment, AI can provide valuable initial insights, but always maintain human oversight for crucial decisions.[3] Use AI-generated feedback as a starting point, then add your personal touch and contextual understanding.[3] This hybrid approach allows you to provide more detailed feedback to more students while maintaining the quality and authenticity of your assessments.

Here are some key principles for maintaining ethical AI workflows:

- Always review AI-generated content before sharing it with students
- Be transparent about when and how AI tools are being used.[1, 2, 3, 4]
- Design assignments that emphasize process and creativity over final products[2, 3, 4]
- Regularly discuss AI ethics and digital citizenship with your students[1, 2, 3, 4]

Remember to collect data on how your AI workflow is impacting both teaching efficiency and student learning outcomes.[2, 3, 4] This doesn't need to be complicated; simple observations about time saved, student engagement levels, and quality of work can provide valuable insights for refining your approach.

Perhaps most importantly, don't feel pressured to transform everything overnight. As research shows, teachers who successfully integrate AI typically start with small, manageable changes and gradually expand their use as their comfort and confidence grow.

Finally, make reflection and continuous improvement part of your workflow.[2, 3, 4] Set aside time regularly to evaluate what's working and what isn't. Share your experiences with colleagues; both successes and challenges.[2, 4] This collaborative approach not only helps you refine your practices but also builds a supportive community around effective AI integration.

Remember, you're not just using AI; you're modeling responsible technology use for your students.[1, 2] By thoughtfully designing your AI workflow, you're preparing them for a future where AI literacy will be as fundamental as reading and writing.[1, 2, 3] And isn't that what great teaching has always been about? Preparing our students for the world they'll inherit while preserving the human elements that make education meaningful. As we conclude our exploration of essential AI teaching tools and workflows, let's take a moment to reflect on the journey we've taken together through this chapter. We've moved from understanding how to evaluate and select AI tools, to discovering core applications for content creation and assessment, to building sustainable workflows that actually work in real classroom settings.

Like Blake Thompson's story taught us at the beginning of this chapter, success with AI tools isn't about adopting every shiny new technology; it's about thoughtfully selecting and implementing tools that genuinely enhance our teaching while respecting our time and our students' needs. We've learned that a streamlined AI toolkit, carefully chosen and masterfully implemented, can transform our teaching practice without overwhelming us or our students.

Let's review the key takeaways from this chapter:

- Start small and focus on tools that address your most pressing needs
- Always prioritize student privacy and data security when selecting AI tools
- Build workflows that enhance rather than complicate your existing teaching practices
- Remember that AI tools should support, not replace, your professional judgment
- Keep the focus on student learning and engagement, not just efficiency

As you begin implementing these tools and strategies in your own classroom, remember that you don't need to revolutionize everything overnight. Start with one tool, master it, then gradually expand your AI toolkit as your confidence grows. The goal isn't to become a tech expert; it's to become a more effective teacher who uses technology wisely.

In the next chapter, we'll explore how to design writing assignments that leverage AI tools while maintaining academic integrity and fostering genuine learning. But for now, take some time to reflect on which AI tools might best serve your specific teaching context. Remember, you're not alone in this journey; thousands of teachers are navigating these same waters, finding ways to harness AI's potential while preserving the human elements that make teaching meaningful.

You've got this. One tool at a time, one lesson at a time, you're building a future-ready classroom that serves both you and your students better. And isn't that what great teaching has always been about?

Reflection Questions:

- Which AI tool discussed in this chapter seems most relevant to your immediate teaching needs?
- What's one specific workflow you could implement next week to save time and enhance learning?
- How might you adapt these tools and strategies to better serve your unique student population?

As you move forward, remember that technology should serve your teaching goals, not dictate them. Trust your professional judgment, start small, and keep your focus on what matters most: creating meaningful learning experiences for your students. The future of AI-enhanced teaching isn't about replacing teachers; it's about empowering us to do what we do best, more effectively and efficiently than ever before.

Chapter 3:

Beyond Language Models: Designing AI-Enhanced Writing Assignments

The morning I discovered three of my top students had used AI tools to write their analysis essays, I realized something crucial: our writing assignments needed to evolve, not dissolve, in the face of AI. Rather than trying to outsmart the technology, we needed to reimagine how writing assignments could harness AI's capabilities while still developing essential critical thinking and communication skills. It was a pivotal moment that made me realize we needed a fundamental shift in our approach to student writing in the AI age. Like many of you, I initially saw AI writing tools as a threat to authentic student learning. But as I began exploring these tools alongside my students, I discovered something surprising: when thoughtfully integrated, AI could actually deepen student engagement with writing rather than diminish it.

Emily's story resonates deeply with this transformation. As a veteran AP Literature teacher with fifteen years of experience, she faced the AI writing challenge head-on when she noticed her students' essays becoming technically flawless but eerily void of personal voice and analytical depth. Rather than fighting against the tide, she developed her innovative "Personal Connection Framework" that revolutionized how her students approached writing.

By shifting from traditional literary analysis to assignments that demanded personal connections and contemporary parallels, Emily found a way to make AI a partner in the writing process rather than a shortcut around it. Her students used AI tools for brainstorming and initial idea generation while maintaining their authentic voices in the final product. The results were remarkable; not only did student engagement increase, but the quality of analytical thinking deepened as students learned to weave their personal experiences with textual analysis.

This chapter will explore how we can follow Emily's lead in redesigning writing assignments that embrace AI as a tool for enhancement rather than replacement. We'll examine practical strategies for crafting prompts that resist generic AI responses, methods for incorporating AI as a writing coach, and assessment approaches that focus on the development of student voice and critical thinking.

As we dive into these strategies, remember that our goal isn't to outsmart AI; it's to harness its potential while preserving what matters most: our students' ability to think deeply, express themselves authentically, and develop their unique voices as writers. The future of writing instruction isn't about choosing between tradition and technology - it's about thoughtfully blending both to create more meaningful learning experiences.

Whether you're just beginning to explore AI writing tools or looking to refine your existing approach, this chapter will provide you with concrete strategies to transform your writing assignments for the AI age. Let's embrace this opportunity to reimagine writing instruction in ways that both challenge and support our students' growth as writers and thinkers.

Crafting AI-Resistant Writing Prompts: Moving Beyond Generic Questions

Let's be honest; we've all seen those writing prompts that practically beg students to copy-paste from AI. You know the ones: "Analyze the themes in The Great Gatsby" or "Explain the causes of the Civil War." These generic questions might have worked in 2020, but in today's AI-powered world, they're about as effective as asking students not to use calculators for basic math.[2]

The good news? We can design writing assignments that not only resist AI completion but also lead to deeper learning and more authentic student engagement. The key is moving beyond surface-level questions to prompts that demand personal connection, specific context, and original thinking.[2, 16]

Let's start with what makes a prompt AI-resistant. First, it should require students to draw on experiences or knowledge that AI can't access. Think classroom discussions, personal reflections, or local community connections. Second, it should emphasize process over product, asking students to document their thinking journey rather than just deliver a polished final draft. Finally, it should promote synthesis and original thought rather than simple information retrieval.[2, 16]

Here are some practical strategies for transforming traditional prompts into AI-resistant ones:

- Instead of "Discuss the themes in *Hamlet*," try "How does Hamlet's relationship with his father mirror or contrast your own experience with family expectations?"
- Rather than "Explain the causes of climate change," ask "How have recent weather events in our community reflected the climate patterns we've studied? What local solutions could address these challenges?"
- Instead of "Analyze the author's use of symbolism," try "Choose a symbol from our class discussion that resonated with you personally. How does your interpretation differ from those shared by your classmates?"

The magic happens when we combine these personal connections with process documentation. Ask students to submit their brainstorming notes, early drafts, and revision reflections alongside their final work. This not only makes AI shortcuts less tempting but also helps students develop metacognitive skills.[16]

Multimodal assignments add another layer of AI resistance. When we ask students to create infographics, record podcast episodes, or design visual presentations alongside their writing, we're requiring forms of expression that current AI tools struggle to replicate. Plus, these varied formats often engage students who might otherwise find traditional essays daunting.[2, 16]

Collaboration can be another powerful tool in our AI-resistant arsenal. Group projects that require documented discussion, peer feedback, and collective problem-solving make it much harder for students to rely solely on AI-generated content. When students must explain their thinking to peers and negotiate different viewpoints, they're developing skills that AI simply can't replicate.[16]

But here's what's really exciting: AI-resistant prompts often lead to more engaging and meaningful work. When students connect course content to their lived experiences, they're not just avoiding AI shortcuts; they're developing a deeper understanding and more authentic voices as writers.[2]

Remember, the goal isn't to make assignments so complex that students can't use AI at all. Instead, we want to create prompts where AI becomes a helpful tool rather than a replacement for student thinking. Consider allowing students to use AI for brainstorming or editing while requiring clear evidence of their own analysis and reflection.[2, 16]

As you redesign your writing prompts, keep these guiding questions in mind:

- Does this prompt require knowledge of specific class discussions or activities?
- Can students meaningfully connect the topic to their personal experiences?
- Does the assignment document the thinking process, not just the final product?
- Are students asked to synthesize multiple sources or perspectives?
- Does the prompt encourage original, creative thinking?

By focusing on these elements, we can create writing assignments that not only resist AI completion but also help our students become stronger, more confident writers. The future of writing instruction isn't about outsmarting AI; it's about using it wisely while preserving what matters most: our students' authentic voices and critical thinking skills.[2, 16]

Integrating AI as a Writing Coach: From Brainstorming to Revision

Think of AI as that enthusiastic student teacher who's always ready to help but needs clear direction from you, the experienced educator. When thoughtfully integrated into the writing process, AI can serve as a tireless writing coach that supports, rather than replaces, student thinking and creativity.[17, 18, 19]

Let's explore how AI can enhance each stage of the writing process while maintaining our commitment to developing authentic student voices. The key is understanding exactly when and how to leverage AI tools effectively.[17, 18]

At the brainstorming stage, AI can serve as an idea generator and thought partner. Tools like PapyrusAI can help students explore different angles on their topic, suggest relevant examples, and identify potential counterarguments.[18, 19] But here's the crucial part: we want students using AI to expand their thinking, not replace it. Have students start with their own initial ideas, then use AI to probe deeper or consider new perspectives they hadn't thought of.[18]

For example, if a student is writing about climate change, they might begin by sharing their main argument with an AI writing coach. The AI can then prompt them to consider opposing viewpoints, suggest local examples to strengthen their case, or highlight potential biases in their thinking.[18] This scaffolded approach helps students develop critical thinking skills while maintaining ownership of their ideas.[18, 19]

During the drafting phase, AI can provide real-time feedback on organization, clarity, and coherence.[17, 19] But remember, we're using AI as a coach, not a ghostwriter. Set clear guidelines for students about using AI to strengthen their own writing rather than generating content for them.[17, 19] Have them document their AI interactions and reflect on how the feedback shaped their choices.[18]

Here are some practical strategies for integrating AI coaching effectively:

- Require students to submit their original brainstorming notes before engaging with AI tools[18]
- Have students maintain a revision log documenting specific changes made based on AI feedback[18]
- Create checkpoints where students share their writing with both AI and peer reviewers, then compare the different types of feedback[18]
- Ask students to reflect on how AI suggestions influenced their thinking and what they chose to accept or reject[18]

The revision stage is where AI coaching can be particularly powerful. Modern AI writing tools can provide instant, neutral feedback on everything from grammar and style to argument strength and evidence use.[17, 18, 19] But here's where your expertise as an educator becomes crucial; help students learn to evaluate AI suggestions critically rather than accepting them unquestioningly.[17, 19]

Research from Utah State University's AI writing coach pilot program shows that when students are taught to use AI tools thoughtfully, they develop stronger critical thinking skills and more confidence in their writing.[18] The key finding? Students who used AI as a collaborative tool rather than a crutch showed the most improvement.[18]

But let's be honest, implementing AI coaching requires careful planning and clear boundaries. Here are some guardrails to consider:

- Establish specific guidelines for when and how students should use AI tools during each writing stage[17, 18]
- Create rubrics that assess both the final product and the student's process, including their thoughtful use of AI feedback[18]
- Require transparency about AI use through documentation and reflection[18]
- Monitor student-AI interactions to ensure meaningful engagement[18]

Remember, our goal isn't to create AI-dependent writers, but to help students become more confident, skilled, and independent authors who know how to leverage AI tools effectively.[17, 19] When implemented thoughtfully, AI writing coaches can provide the kind of individualized attention and immediate feedback that we wish we could give every student, every time they write.[17, 18]

The future of writing instruction isn't about choosing between human and artificial intelligence; it's about finding the sweet spot where technology enhances rather than replaces student thinking.[17, 18, 19] As you begin integrating AI coaching into your writing instruction, start small, be clear about expectations, and always keep the focus on developing student voice and critical thinking skills.[17, 19]

You've got this! And remember, you're not replacing yourself as a writing teacher; you're adding a powerful tool to your instructional toolkit that can help every student become a stronger, more confident writer.[17, 18, 19]

Assessment Strategies for AI-Enhanced Writing: Focusing on Process Over Product

Let's be honest; if you're like most writing teachers, you've probably spent countless hours agonizing over how to fairly assess student work in an AI world. The finished essay sitting in your inbox might look polished, but how do you know what your student actually learned? This is where process-focused assessment becomes your secret weapon.[20, 23]

The key shift we need to make is moving our assessment lens from the final product to the journey of writing itself. Research from leading educational institutions confirms that when we emphasize the writing process, we not only get a clearer picture of student learning but also make it harder to rely solely on AI-generated content.[20, 23]

Here are some practical strategies for making this shift:

- Require process portfolios that include drafts, outlines, and revision notes[20, 21]
- Ask students to maintain AI use logs documenting when and how they used AI tools[23]
- Incorporate regular reflection points where students analyze their writing choices[22, 23]
- Use collaborative writing projects that highlight both individual and group contributions[20, 22]

One of the most powerful approaches is implementing what I call the "transparency framework." This involves creating clear categories for AI use in assignments:[23]

- No AI permitted: For specific skills assessment
- Limited AI use: Allowing tools for brainstorming or editing only
- Full AI integration: Requiring documented AI collaboration

The magic happens when we make these categories explicit and teach students how to document their AI interactions thoughtfully. This isn't about policing their writing; it's about helping them become more aware and intentional writers.[22, 23]

Metacognition becomes our best friend in this process. When we ask students to reflect on their writing journey, including how they used AI tools, we gain invaluable insights into their thinking and decision-making. These reflections often reveal more about student learning than the final essay ever could.[22, 23]

But let's talk about what this looks like in practice. Instead of just grading the final research paper, consider creating checkpoints throughout the writing process:[20, 21]

- Initial brainstorming documentation
- Outline with sources and reasoning
- Draft with revision notes
- AI interaction log (if permitted)
- Final reflection on writing choices

This approach not only makes assessment more authentic but also helps students develop crucial skills in planning, revision, and critical thinking. Research shows that students who engage in documented reflection and process work demonstrate stronger writing skills and a better understanding of course content.[20, 22, 23]

Here's another game-changing strategy: peer and self-assessment. When students critique each other's work and reflect on their own writing process, they develop a deeper understanding of what makes writing effective. Plus, these interactions are inherently human and can't be replicated by AI.[20, 22]

But what about the practical reality of managing all this documentation? This is where digital platforms become your allies. Learning management systems can help track multiple drafts, AI tools can provide instant feedback on works in progress, and digital portfolios can organize student reflections.[20, 21]

Remember, the goal isn't to make assessment more complicated; it's to make it more meaningful. By focusing on process over product, we're not just adapting to an AI world; we're helping students become more thoughtful, intentional writers.[20, 23]

Here's a simple framework to get started:

- Begin with one assignment where you'll pilot process-focused assessment
- Choose 2-3 specific process elements to track (drafts, reflections, peer feedback)
- Create clear guidelines for how students should document their work
- Design rubrics that value process as much as product[20, 22, 23]

The beauty of this approach is that it naturally promotes academic integrity while supporting genuine learning. When students know they'll be assessed on their process, not just their product, they're more likely to engage meaningfully with the writing task rather than seeking shortcuts.[20, 23]

You've got this! Start small, be clear with your expectations, and remember that shifting to process-focused assessment isn't just about adapting to AI; it's about better teaching and learning. Your students will thank you for helping them become more confident, capable writers who understand both the power and limitations of AI tools in their writing process.[22, 23]As we conclude this chapter on designing AI-enhanced writing assignments, let's pause to reflect on our journey. We began with that heart-stopping moment of discovering AI-generated essays in our classrooms and transformed it into an opportunity to revolutionize how we teach writing. Through Emily's story and our exploration of AI-resistant prompts, coaching strategies, and process-focused assessment, we've discovered that AI doesn't have to be the enemy of authentic writing—it can be a powerful ally.

The key takeaways are clear: effective writing instruction in the AI age requires us to shift our focus from polished final products to meaningful processes, from generic prompts to personally connected assignments, and from traditional assessment methods to more holistic evaluation approaches. By embracing these changes, we're not just adapting to new technology; we're creating more engaging and authentic writing experiences for our students.

Remember those three students whose AI-generated essays sparked this conversation? They taught us something invaluable: when faced with technological change, we can either resist or reimagine. By choosing to reimagine, we've discovered ways to harness AI's potential while preserving what matters most: our students' voices, their critical thinking skills, and their growth as writers.

As you begin implementing these strategies in your own classroom, start small. Perhaps begin with redesigning one writing assignment using the Personal Connection Framework we discussed. Or experiment with using AI as a brainstorming tool while maintaining strict documentation requirements. Whatever your starting point, remember that you're not trying to outsmart AI; you're teaching students how to use it wisely while developing their own unique voices.

In the next chapter, we'll explore how to extend these principles beyond writing assignments into the broader realm of research and digital literacy. But for now, take a moment to celebrate how far you've come. You're not just teaching writing in the AI age; you're helping shape how the next generation will think, create, and express themselves in a world where human and artificial intelligence increasingly intersect.

You've got this, and your students are lucky to have a teacher who's willing to embrace innovation while holding firm to what matters most: their growth as thinkers and writers.

Chapter 4:

Research in the AI Age: Teaching Digital Literacy and Critical Thinking

Digital literacy in the AI age requires more than just teaching students how to spot fake news or evaluate website credibility; it demands a complete reimagining of what it means to be a critical thinker in a world where information is increasingly AI-generated. As I watched my students navigate through a sea of AI-created content last semester, I realized we needed to develop a new framework for research that embraces both technological innovation and traditional academic values. Today's students are navigating an increasingly complex digital landscape where the line between human and machine-generated content grows ever thinner. As educators, we must evolve our teaching approaches to help students develop the critical thinking skills needed to evaluate, analyze, and effectively use AI-enhanced research tools.

Ivy's story resonates deeply with many of us who have witnessed the transformation of student research habits in recent years. Teaching at Lincoln High School, she noticed a troubling pattern in her students' work. Their citations were perfect, their formatting flawless, but their analysis lacked depth. After discovering that many were relying heavily on AI research assistants, she developed what she called the

"Three-Layer Research Method." The first layer involved traditional database searches, the second incorporated AI tools for initial analysis, and the third required students to synthesize findings through their own critical lens. She tested this approach with her AP History class, asking them to research local civil rights movements. The results were remarkable; students began using AI to efficiently gather initial data but then went deeper, conducting original interviews and analyzing primary sources to verify and expand upon AI-generated insights. One student discovered that an AI-suggested "fact" about a local protest was actually incorrect, leading to a valuable class discussion about the importance of human verification in research. By the end of the semester, Ivy's students weren't just better researchers; they had become more discerning digital citizens who understood both the potential and limitations of AI in academic research.

Ivy's experience highlights a crucial truth: teaching digital literacy in the AI age requires a delicate balance between embracing technological innovation and maintaining rigorous academic standards. We must help our students understand that while AI can be an incredibly powerful research assistant, it should never replace human curiosity, critical thinking, and the joy of authentic discovery.

In this chapter, we'll explore practical strategies for teaching students to navigate this new research landscape. We'll examine methods for evaluating AI-generated content, techniques for developing robust research skills, and approaches to creating assignments that promote genuine inquiry. Most importantly, we'll discuss how to help students become confident, ethical researchers who can harness AI's capabilities while maintaining their academic integrity.

As we delve into these crucial topics, remember that our goal isn't to fight against AI technology, but to embrace it as a tool for enhancing student learning while preserving the fundamental skills that make research meaningful and valuable. Let's explore how we can guide our students to become thoughtful, discerning researchers in this rapidly evolving digital age.

Teaching Source Evaluation in an AI-Generated World

In today's digital landscape, teaching students to evaluate sources has become both more critical and more complex than ever before. The challenge isn't just helping students distinguish between reliable and unreliable sources; it's teaching them to navigate a world where AI can generate convincing academic papers, create realistic-looking citations, and produce content that's increasingly difficult to distinguish from human-written work.[1, 2, 3]

Let's start with a fundamental truth: AI literacy is now an essential component of source evaluation. Our students need to understand not just how to evaluate traditional sources, but also how to recognize and assess AI-generated content.[1, 3] This means going beyond the traditional CRAAP Test (Currency, Relevance, Authority, Accuracy, Purpose) to develop new frameworks that account for the unique challenges of AI-generated information.[2, 3]

One effective approach is to teach students the "Triple V" method: Verify, Validate, and Value. When students encounter any source, especially one they suspect might be AI-generated, they should:

- Verify: Cross-reference information with multiple reliable sources
- Validate: Check for citations and trace them back to their origins
- Value: Assess the unique human perspective or original research that makes the source valuable

This framework helps students develop a healthy skepticism while giving them practical tools for evaluation. Remember, our goal isn't to make students fear AI-generated content but to help them become discerning consumers of information in all its forms.[2, 3]

A crucial aspect of teaching source evaluation in the AI age is transparency. We need to encourage students to be open about their use of AI tools and to document their research process.[1] This isn't just about academic honesty; it's about developing good research habits that will serve them well beyond the classroom.

One particularly effective strategy is to incorporate source evaluation workshops where students analyze both human-created and AI-generated materials side by side. This hands-on experience helps them develop the critical thinking skills needed to identify potential red flags in AI-generated content, such as plausible-sounding but inaccurate information or fabricated citations.[1, 3]

It's also important to address the ethical dimensions of using AI in research. Students need to understand that while AI can be a powerful research assistant, it shouldn't replace human critical thinking and original analysis.[2, 3] We can demonstrate this by designing assignments that require students to engage with primary sources, conduct local research, or document their reasoning process; tasks that are more challenging for AI to replicate convincingly.[2, 3]

Remember, we're not just teaching students how to evaluate sources; we're preparing them to be ethical, discerning researchers in a world where the line between human and machine-generated content continues to blur.[1, 2, 3] By embedding these skills into our curriculum, we help students develop the digital literacy they need to succeed in their academic careers and beyond.

Practical Tips for Teaching Source Evaluation:

- Create transparency protocols requiring students to document their research process, including any AI tools used.[1]
- Design assignments that combine traditional research methods with careful evaluation of AI-generated content.[2, 3]
- Incorporate regular discussions about the ethical implications of using AI in research.[2, 3]
- Use real examples of AI-generated misinformation to build critical evaluation skills.[3]

As we guide our students through this new terrain, it's crucial to maintain a balance between embracing technological innovation and preserving the fundamental skills that make research meaningful.[2] The goal isn't to avoid AI-generated content entirely but to help students understand when and how to use it appropriately while maintaining their academic integrity.[1]

Remember, you don't need to be an AI expert to teach these skills effectively. What matters most is helping students develop a questioning mindset and the confidence to evaluate sources critically, whether they're created by humans or machines.[2, 3] By focusing on these fundamental skills, we prepare our students not just for academic success, but for lifelong learning in an AI-enhanced world.[1, 2, 3]

Developing Critical Research Skills: Balancing AI Tools with Human Insight

Let's be honest; teaching research skills has never been more challenging. Our students have AI research assistants in their pockets that can generate citations, summarize articles, and even draft literature reviews in seconds.[1, 2] But here's the good news: we can teach our students to harness these powerful tools while developing the critical thinking skills they'll need for life beyond our classrooms.

The key is understanding that AI should be a research partner, not a replacement for human insight.[1, 2, 24] Think of AI as a really efficient research assistant; one that can help gather initial information and suggest connections, but that needs human oversight to ensure accuracy and depth. This perspective helps us strike that crucial balance between embracing innovation and maintaining academic rigor.

Here are some practical strategies for integrating AI tools while fostering genuine research skills:

- Start with AI-assisted brainstorming, but require students to justify their chosen research directions using human reasoning
- Use fact-checking exercises where students verify AI-provided information against academic databases
- Incorporate comparative analysis between AI-generated summaries and traditional research methods

One of the most effective approaches is what I call the "Research Process Portfolio." Instead of just evaluating final papers, have students document their entire research journey.[2, 3] This includes how they used AI tools, what information they accepted or rejected, and most importantly, why. This approach shifts the focus from the product to the process, helping students develop critical thinking skills while using AI responsibly.

When it comes to assessment, consider designing assignments that require students to go beyond what AI can easily provide.[2, 3] For example:

- Require personal reflections on how sources connect to students' own experiences
- Ask for oral presentations where students defend their research choices
- Include primary source analysis or local research components

Remember, our goal isn't to make students fear AI or avoid it entirely; it's to help them become discerning researchers who can effectively combine technological tools with human judgment.[1, 2] This means teaching them to ask good questions, verify information, and think critically about both AI-generated and traditional sources.

One particularly effective strategy is to incorporate regular "AI Insight Checks" into your research units.[3] Have students compare AI-generated summaries with their own analysis of sources, identifying what the AI might have missed or misinterpreted. This helps develop that crucial skill of critical evaluation while acknowledging AI's role in modern research.

To protect academic integrity while embracing AI tools, establish clear guidelines around transparency and documentation.[3] Have students:

- Document which AI tools they used and how
- Explain their verification process for AI-generated information
- Reflect on how AI assisted their research process

The key to success is maintaining a balance between efficiency and depth.[1, 2, 3] Yes, AI can help students gather information more quickly, but we need to ensure they're still developing those essential critical thinking muscles. Encourage students to use AI for initial exploration, but require them to dig deeper through traditional research methods, primary source analysis, and original synthesis.

Remember, you don't need to be an AI expert to guide students through this process.[3] What matters most is helping them develop a questioning mindset and the confidence to evaluate sources critically, whether they're created by humans or machines. By focusing on these fundamental skills, we prepare our students not just for academic success, but for lifelong learning in an AI-enhanced world.

As you implement these strategies, stay flexible and open to adjustment. What works for one class might need tweaking for another. The goal is to find that sweet spot where AI tools enhance rather than replace the development of genuine research skills.[1, 2, 24] Trust your professional judgment; you know your students best.

By embracing this balanced approach, we can help our students become confident, ethical researchers who know how to leverage AI while maintaining their academic integrity and critical thinking skills.[1, 2, 3] That's not just good teaching; it's preparing them for the future they'll inherit.

Creating Authentic Research Projects That Promote Digital Literacy

Creating authentic research projects in the AI age requires a delicate balance between leveraging digital tools and fostering genuine inquiry skills. We're not just teaching students how to use technology; we're helping them become discerning digital citizens who can navigate an increasingly complex information landscape with confidence and integrity.[29]

Let's start with a fundamental principle: authentic research projects should mirror real-world practices while connecting to students' lives and interests. This isn't just about assigning a research paper; it's about designing experiences that engage students in meaningful inquiry using the digital tools and methods that professionals use in their fields.[27, 28]

Here are key elements to consider when designing authentic research projects:

- Connect projects to real-world issues or student interests to increase relevance and motivation
- Mirror professional practices by incorporating digital tools that experts actually use
- Encourage student choice in both topic selection and presentation format
- Require sustained inquiry and reflection throughout the research process.[27, 28]

One effective approach is to integrate Project-Based Learning (PBL) with digital literacy skills. This combination helps students develop both research capabilities and the critical thinking skills needed to evaluate online sources.[27] For example, when students investigate local community issues, they learn to use digital tools for data collection while developing real-world research skills.

Scaffolding digital literacy skills is crucial for student success. Start with explicit instruction in digital research methods: how to evaluate sources, use search engines effectively, understand digital footprints, and cite sources ethically. Partner with your school librarian or media specialist to co-teach these skills.[27, 29] Remember, we're building a foundation that students will use throughout their academic careers and beyond.

Here's a practical framework for designing authentic research projects that promote digital literacy:

- Begin with a compelling question or problem that matters to students
- Teach explicit digital research skills before diving into independent work
- Offer choices in both research methods and final presentation formats
- Build in regular checkpoints for source evaluation and reflection
- Include opportunities for peer feedback and revision.[26]

When it comes to assessment, consider both the process and the product. How well did students use digital platforms to conduct their research? Did they effectively evaluate and synthesize information from multiple sources? Did they create something that demonstrates both content mastery and digital literacy?[26]

One particularly effective strategy is to have students document their research journey through what we call a "Digital Research Portfolio." This includes not just their final product, but evidence of their search strategies, source evaluation process, and reflections on their learning.[25] This approach helps students develop metacognitive skills while giving you insight into their research process.

To ensure equity and access, be mindful of students' varying levels of technology access and experience. Provide clear support structures and alternative options when needed.[29] Remember, the goal is to help all students develop these essential skills, not to create additional barriers to learning.

Here are some practical tips for implementation:

- Start small with a pilot project in one unit before scaling up
- Create clear rubrics that assess both content knowledge and digital literacy skills
- Build in time for students to share their work with authentic audiences
- Document successful strategies to share with colleagues.[26, 28]

Remember, you don't need to be a technology expert to guide students through this process. What matters most is helping them develop the critical thinking skills needed to navigate digital information effectively.[29] Trust your teaching instincts; you already know how to guide students through complex learning tasks.

By focusing on authentic research experiences that promote digital literacy, we're not just teaching students how to complete assignments; we're preparing them for success in an increasingly digital world.[25, 27] When we combine thoughtful project design with explicit instruction in digital skills, we create powerful learning opportunities that engage students while building essential competencies for their future.

As you implement these strategies, stay flexible and open to adjustment. What works for one class might need tweaking for another. The goal is to find approaches that work for your students while maintaining high standards for both research quality and digital literacy development.

Remember, this isn't about replacing traditional research skills; it's about enhancing them with digital tools and strategies that reflect how research is actually conducted in the modern world.[25] By embracing this approach, we help our students become confident, ethical researchers who can effectively navigate both digital and traditional sources of information. As we conclude this chapter on research in the AI age, let's take a moment to reflect on the transformative journey we've explored. We began with Ivy's story of helping her students navigate the complex intersection of traditional research methods and AI tools. Her experience reminds us that teaching digital literacy isn't just about mastering new technologies; it's about fostering critical thinking skills that will serve our students well beyond the classroom.

Through our exploration of source evaluation, critical research skills, and authentic project design, we've discovered that AI can be a powerful ally in research when used thoughtfully and ethically. The key insights we've uncovered include:

- Teaching students to be discerning evaluators of both AI-generated and traditional sources
- Developing research frameworks that combine AI efficiency with human insight
- Creating authentic projects that engage students in meaningful inquiry while building digital literacy
- Maintaining academic integrity through transparency and documented research processes

As we look ahead, remember that you don't need to implement everything at once. Start small, perhaps with one research unit where you introduce the "Triple V" method or experiment with the Research

Process Portfolio. Pay attention to what works for your students and adjust accordingly.

One of my favorite moments as an educator came last semester when a student stopped by my desk after completing our first AI-enhanced research project. "You know," she said, "I thought using AI would make research easier, but it actually made me think more carefully about my sources." That's exactly the kind of critical awareness we're aiming to develop.

As you return to your classroom, remember that you're not just teaching research skills; you're preparing students to be thoughtful, ethical participants in an increasingly digital world. Your expertise and guidance matter more than ever as students learn to navigate this new landscape.

In the next chapter, we'll explore practical strategies for saving time with AI while maintaining the quality of our teaching. But for now, take a moment to appreciate how far you've come in understanding and teaching research skills in the AI age. You're already helping your students develop the critical thinking abilities they'll need for success in both academic and professional contexts.

Remember, the goal isn't to fight against AI or to embrace it unquestioningly; it's to help our students become confident, discerning researchers who can effectively use all the tools at their disposal while maintaining their academic integrity and intellectual curiosity. As we move forward, let's continue to explore, experiment, and share our successes and challenges with fellow educators.

You've got this, and your students are fortunate to have a teacher who cares enough to guide them through this important transition in how we approach research and learning. Keep experimenting, stay curious, and trust your professional judgment as you help your students navigate this exciting new frontier in education.

Chapter 5:

Time-Saving AI Strategies: Work Smarter, Not Harder

Time is every teacher's most precious and scarce resource; I've never met an educator who said, "You know what? I just have too many free hours in my day." As we explore AI-powered time-saving strategies, remember that our goal isn't to automate teaching away, but to eliminate the repetitive tasks that drain our energy so we can focus on what truly matters: meaningful interactions with our students. The truth is, most of us became teachers to make a difference in our students' lives, not to become efficiency experts. Yet here we are, facing ever-growing demands on our time and energy while trying to maintain the quality of education our students deserve.

In this chapter, we'll explore how AI can become your personal teaching assistant, helping you reclaim precious hours without compromising the heart of what makes your teaching meaningful. We'll dive into practical strategies that real teachers are using to streamline their workflows, enhance their effectiveness, and yes, actually leave school at a reasonable hour.

Last spring, I found myself drowning in end-of-semester responsibilities. Between grading final projects, writing report card comments, and planning for next year, I was averaging five hours of sleep and still falling behind. One particularly exhausting Sunday, while creating yet another rubric from scratch, I realized I was repeating work I'd done dozens of times before. That's when I decided to experiment with AI as my personal teaching assistant. I started small, using AI to help generate rubric criteria based on my previous assessments. Then I expanded to using it for creating differentiated writing prompts and personalizing feedback templates. Within weeks, I had cut my planning time in half.

The real breakthrough came when I developed what I call my "AI Enhancement System," a collection of proven prompts and workflows that helped me tackle common teaching tasks efficiently. By the end of the semester, I wasn't just surviving; I was leaving school at a reasonable hour and actually had energy for my family. The time I saved went right back into what I loved most: having meaningful conversations with students about their work and innovating new teaching approaches. This wasn't about cutting corners; it was about working smarter to be more present and effective as an educator.

Through this chapter, we'll explore systematic approaches to integrating AI into your daily routine, focusing on three key areas: lesson planning and resource creation, assessment and feedback, and administrative tasks. You'll learn specific strategies for using AI to enhance your efficiency while maintaining the quality and personal touch that make your teaching unique.

Remember, the goal isn't to automate away the human elements of teaching; it's to eliminate the repetitive tasks that drain our energy so we can focus more on what truly matters: those meaningful moments of connection and discovery with our students. Let's explore how to make AI work for you, not the other way around.

AI-Powered Lesson Planning and Resource Creation: Building Your Template Library

Let's talk about one of the most powerful ways AI can transform your teaching practice: building a personalized template library for lesson planning and resource creation. Think of it as creating your own digital filing cabinet; one that's actually organized, instantly searchable, and adaptable for any teaching scenario you encounter. [2, 30, 31]

The beauty of using AI for lesson planning isn't just about saving time (though that's a huge benefit). It's about creating a foundation of high-quality resources that you can customize and improve over time. [30] Remember those late nights spent recreating worksheets you know you made last year, but can't find? Or the frustration of adapting a great lesson plan for different learning levels? AI can help eliminate these common pain points. [30, 31]

Let's start with the basics of building your template library. First, you'll want to create what I call your "core prompts," these are your go-to AI requests that consistently produce useful results. [31] For example:

- Lesson outline generators that include objectives, activities, and assessment ideas
- Differentiation templates that help modify content for various learning levels

- Rubric creators that align with your teaching standards
- Activity generators for different learning styles

The key is to start small and build gradually. Choose one type of resource you frequently create, maybe it's writing prompts or discussion questions, and focus on developing effective AI prompts for that specific need.[31] As you become comfortable, expand your template library to include more complex resources.

One crucial aspect of building an effective template library is organization. Create clear categories for your templates based on:

- Subject area or unit
- Skill focus (critical thinking, analysis, research, etc.)
- Student level or needed modifications
- Assessment type

Remember, AI is your assistant, not your replacement.[30] The most effective approach is to use AI-generated content as a starting point, then apply your professional judgment to refine and personalize the materials.[30, 31] This is where your expertise as an educator becomes invaluable; you know your students, their needs, and your curriculum requirements better than any AI tool ever could.

When working with AI to create resources, always keep these best practices in mind:

- Review and adapt all AI-generated content to ensure it's appropriate for your students.[30, 31]
- Maintain transparency about AI use in your planning process.[2, 30]

- Regularly evaluate resources for potential bias or accessibility issues.[30]
- Save successful prompts and templates for future use

One particularly effective strategy is to use AI for creating differentiated versions of your lessons and materials. Instead of spending hours manually adapting content for different learning levels, you can use AI to quickly generate multiple versions while maintaining the core learning objectives.[30] This allows you to provide more personalized support without multiplying your workload.

As you build your template library, you'll likely discover that certain prompts consistently produce better results than others. Keep a record of these "golden prompts" and share them with colleagues who might benefit from them.[30] This collaborative approach not only helps your entire department work more efficiently but also creates opportunities for professional growth and innovation.

Remember, the goal isn't to create a perfect resource the first time; it's to develop a growing collection of adaptable templates that evolve with your teaching practice.[30] Start with what you need most urgently, experiment with different approaches, and gradually expand your library as your confidence with AI tools grows.

By investing time upfront in building your template library, you're creating a valuable resource that will save countless hours throughout your teaching career.[2, 30, 31] More importantly, you're developing a systematic approach to lesson planning that allows you to focus more energy on what really matters: connecting with your students and fostering meaningful learning experiences.

Streamlining Assessment and Feedback with AI Assistance

Assessment and feedback; they're the tasks that keep us up at night, hunched over stacks of papers with our red pens and coffee mugs. But what if AI could help us provide more meaningful feedback while reclaiming some of those precious evening hours? Let's explore how to make AI your assessment ally without compromising the personal touch that makes your feedback valuable.

First, let's acknowledge a fundamental truth: AI isn't meant to replace your professional judgment.[3, 4] Instead, think of it as a smart assistant that can handle the repetitive aspects of assessment, freeing you to focus on the nuanced feedback that only a human teacher can provide. The goal is to work smarter, not harder, while maintaining, or even improving, the quality of feedback our students receive.

One particularly powerful approach is using AI to create what I call "feedback frameworks,"

customized templates that help you provide consistent, detailed responses across different types of assignments. These frameworks can include:

- Common writing issues and suggested improvements
- Subject-specific terminology and concepts
- Differentiated explanation levels for various student needs
- Links to additional resources and practice materials

The key to effective AI-assisted feedback is maintaining that crucial balance between efficiency and personalization. Start by using AI to handle the routine elements of assessment, like checking for basic grammar errors or identifying missing components in an assignment.[3, 4] This creates a foundation that you can build upon with your own insights and observations.

Many educators have found success using AI tools to provide immediate, formative feedback while students are still working on assignments.[32] For instance, platforms that use natural language processing can help students identify areas for improvement in real-time, allowing them to revise their work before final submission. This not only reduces your grading load but also helps students develop stronger self-editing skills.

When it comes to rubric-based assessment, AI can be particularly helpful in maintaining consistency across large numbers of assignments.[3] By analyzing student work against detailed rubrics, AI systems can help ensure that every student receives fair and thorough feedback, regardless of when their work is being evaluated. However, it's crucial to remember that these systems should support, not supplant, your professional judgment.

Here are some practical strategies for integrating AI into your assessment workflow:

- Use AI to generate initial feedback drafts that you can then personalize.
- Leverage analytics to identify class-wide trends and inform targeted interventions.[4, 32]
- Create a bank of common feedback responses that can be quickly customized.

- Set up automated systems for routine checks while reserving your energy for deeper analysis.

One of the most powerful aspects of AI-assisted assessment is its ability to provide immediate, actionable feedback to students.[32] Research has shown that feedback is most effective when it's timely and specific, something that's challenging to achieve consistently with traditional grading methods. With AI support, you can provide that immediate response while still maintaining the quality and personal touch that makes your feedback meaningful.

However, it's essential to maintain transparency with your students about how AI tools are being used in the assessment process.[4, 16] This not only builds trust but also helps students understand how to interpret and act on the feedback they receive. Remember to regularly review AI-generated feedback for accuracy and fairness, keeping in mind that these tools can sometimes inherit biases from their training data.

As you implement these strategies, start small and build gradually. Choose one aspect of your assessment process to enhance with AI, master it, and then expand to other areas. This approach helps prevent overwhelm while ensuring that you're using these tools effectively and ethically.[16]

Remember, the goal isn't to automate away the human elements of assessment; it's to enhance our ability to provide meaningful feedback that helps our students grow.[3, 4] By thoughtfully integrating AI into our assessment practices, we can create more opportunities for the kind of deep, personalized feedback that makes a real difference in student learning.

As you explore these tools and strategies, keep in mind that you're not just saving time; you're reimagining how assessment can work in your classroom. With AI as your assistant, you can provide more consistent, timely, and personalized feedback while maintaining the professional judgment and human connection that make you an effective educator.[4, 16]

Creating Sustainable AI Workflows: From Daily Tasks to Long-Term Planning

Creating a sustainable AI workflow isn't just about adopting new tools; it's about developing systems that work for you day after day, week after week, without adding to your cognitive load.[3, 4] Think of it as setting up your classroom at the beginning of the year: you want systems that will serve you well through the ups and downs of the academic calendar.

Let's start with a fundamental truth: the most sustainable workflows are the ones that align with how you actually teach, not how you think you should teach. As Matt Miller notes in *AI for Educators*, "You can't stop teaching until you wrap your brain around AI. Learn about quick changes you can make right now to adjust."[31] This means starting with your current practices and gradually enhancing them with AI support.

Here's a practical framework for building sustainable AI workflows:

- Start with your pain points: Identify tasks that consistently drain your time and energy.[31]

- Choose one task to automate: Focus on mastering one AI workflow before adding others.[31]
- Build in review checkpoints: Schedule regular times to evaluate and adjust your AI systems.[3, 4]
- Document your successes: Keep track of what works to build your confidence and expertise.[31]

One of the most effective approaches is what I call the "AI Task Triage" system. This involves categorizing your teaching tasks into three levels:

- Level 1: Quick wins (daily tasks like email responses and basic feedback)[31]
- Level 2: Strategic support (weekly planning and assessment activities)[31]
- Level 3: Long-term projects (curriculum development and resource creation)[3, 4]

The key to sustainability is starting with Level 1 tasks; the quick wins that give you immediate time savings without requiring major changes to your teaching practice.[31] For instance, using AI to generate initial feedback comments that you can then personalize, or creating templates for routine communications with students and parents.[31]

As you become comfortable with basic AI workflows, you can gradually move into Level 2 tasks. This might include using AI to help differentiate assignments or create scaffolded learning materials for different student needs.[3, 31, 4] Research shows that teachers who take this gradual approach are more likely to sustain their AI integration long-term.

For long-term planning (Level 3), consider creating what we call "AI checkpoints," scheduled times throughout the year when you review and update your AI workflows,[3, 4] This might include:

- Monthly review of AI-generated materials for accuracy and relevance[3, 16]
- Quarterly assessment of time savings and impact on student learning[3, 4]
- Semester planning for new AI integrations based on changing needs.[3]

Remember, sustainability isn't just about efficiency; it's about maintaining the quality and integrity of your teaching while reducing unnecessary workload.[3, 4] As noted in Teaching with AI, "Helping every student believe and experience 'I care, I can, I matter' in an age of AI may be the most important lesson."[3]

One particularly effective strategy is to create what we call an "AI Enhancement System," a collection of proven prompts and workflows that you can rely on repeatedly.[31] This might include:

- Template prompts for common teaching tasks[31, 4]
- Checklists for reviewing AI-generated content[3, 16]
- Guidelines for when to use (and when not to use) AI assistance[3, 16]

The goal is to build a system that becomes second nature, much like your other classroom routines.[31] Just as you have systems for taking attendance or managing classroom discussions, your AI workflows should feel natural and supportive rather than burdensome.[3, 31]

When it comes to long-term planning, think about how AI can support your broader educational goals.[3, 16] This might include:

- Curriculum mapping and unit planning[3, 4]
- Creating differentiated resource banks[31, 4]
- Developing assessment strategies that work with (not against) AI[3, 16]

Remember to build in regular "human checkpoints," moments where you step back and ensure that AI is truly serving your teaching goals, not reshaping them in ways that don't align with your values or your students' needs.[3, 4, 16]

Sustainable AI workflows also require clear boundaries.[3, 16] Decide in advance:

- Which tasks you'll always do manually[3]
- Which tasks you're comfortable automating[31]
- Where you need a hybrid approach[16]

By establishing these boundaries early, you prevent the common pitfall of over-relying on AI or feeling pressured to automate everything.[3, 16] The goal is to find the sweet spot where AI enhances your teaching without compromising your professional judgment or the personal connections that make teaching meaningful.[3, 4, 16]

Remember, creating sustainable AI workflows is a journey, not a destination.[3] Start small, build gradually, and always keep your core teaching values at the center of your decisions.[3, 4] With thoughtful planning and regular evaluation, AI can become a reliable partner in your teaching practice, not just another tech tool that creates more work than it saves.[3, 31, 4] As we wrap up our exploration of time-saving AI strategies, let's take a moment to reflect on our journey through this chapter. We've discovered that AI isn't just about automation; it's about amplification. It's about taking the repetitive tasks that drain our energy and transforming them into opportunities for more meaningful teaching moments.

Through our investigation of lesson planning, assessment, and workflow optimization, we've seen how AI can become a reliable partner in our daily teaching practice. But perhaps the most important lesson isn't about the technology at all; it's about permitting ourselves to work smarter, not harder. Remember, every minute we save on routine tasks is a minute we can spend doing what we do best: connecting with our students, fostering critical thinking, and creating engaging learning experiences.

Let's revisit the key strategies we've explored:

- Building a personalized template library that grows with your teaching practice
- Creating sustainable feedback systems that maintain quality while saving time
- Developing workflows that actually work for your teaching style and needs

As you begin implementing these strategies in your own classroom, remember that this is a journey, not a race. Start small, celebrate your successes, and don't be afraid to adjust your approach as you learn what works best for you and your students.

The goal isn't to become an AI expert; it's to become a more present, effective, and energized teacher. By thoughtfully integrating AI tools into our daily routines, we can reclaim those precious hours that once disappeared into endless grading and planning sessions.

As one teacher in our learning community recently shared, "I used to think using AI meant I was somehow cheating at my job. Now I realize it's helping me be the teacher I always wanted to be; one who has the time and energy to really see and support each student."

Moving forward, I encourage you to experiment with the strategies we've discussed. Start with one small change; maybe it's using AI to generate differentiated writing prompts or create feedback templates. Pay attention to how it affects both your workload and your teaching effectiveness. Remember, every master teacher started as a beginner once.

In our next chapter, we'll explore how to design assignments that not only work alongside AI but actually leverage it to deepen student learning and engagement. But for now, take a moment to imagine what you could do with an extra hour in your day, an extra ounce of energy in your step, and the confidence that comes from knowing you're working smarter, not harder.

You've got this, fellow educator. Here's to reclaiming our time and redirecting it to what matters most; those magical moments of connection and discovery that make teaching the most rewarding profession in the world.

Chapter 6:

Assessment Revolution: Creating AI-Resistant Assignments That Matter

Assessment in the age of AI isn't about trying to outsmart the technology; it's about reimagining what meaningful evaluation looks like in a world where information is instantly accessible. The real question isn't whether students can find the answer, but whether they can think deeply about it, apply it creatively, and connect it to their own experiences. Like many educators, I've witnessed firsthand how assessment has become one of the most challenging aspects of teaching in the AI era. The traditional methods we once relied on, essays, research papers, and even creative writing assignments, suddenly feel vulnerable to AI assistance, leaving many of us questioning how to evaluate student learning authentically.

Now, before you close this chapter in despair, let me share a story about a fellow teacher who changed my perspective on assessment in the AI age. Noah had been teaching Advanced Composition for years when he noticed a troubling pattern; his students were using AI to generate responses to traditional essay prompts, making it increasingly difficult to assess their true understanding. One evening, while reviewing another set of suspiciously perfect essays, he had an epiphany. Instead of fighting against AI, he decided to transform his assessment approach entirely.

He developed what he called the "Living Portfolio" system, where students had to document their thinking process through voice memos, rough drafts, and reflection journals alongside their final work. The breakthrough came when he asked students to connect their analysis of *The Great Gatsby* to current social media influencer culture, requiring them to include personal observations and real-world examples that AI couldn't fabricate.

The results were remarkable; students began producing more original, thoughtful work because they couldn't simply plug a prompt into a generative AI system. They had to engage with the material personally, drawing connections between their lived experiences and the literature. By the end of the semester, Noah wasn't just assessing final products; he was evaluating growth, critical thinking, and authentic engagement. His students weren't just writing better essays; they were becoming better thinkers.

Noah's story illustrates a crucial truth about assessment in the AI age: our goal isn't to make assignments "AI-proof," it's to make them more meaningful. Throughout this chapter, we'll explore practical strategies for creating assessments that don't just measure learning but deepen it. We'll look at how to design assignments that embrace AI's capabilities while ensuring students develop essential critical thinking skills.

Whether you're feeling overwhelmed by AI's impact on assessment or simply looking for fresh approaches to evaluate student learning, this chapter will provide you with concrete tools and strategies you can implement immediately. Together, we'll explore how to create assessments that matter: ones that challenge students to think deeply, connect personally, and demonstrate genuine understanding in ways that no AI can replicate.

So let's roll up our sleeves and reimagine assessment for this new era. It's not about fighting technology; it's about harnessing it to create more meaningful learning experiences for our students.

Designing Performance-Based Assessments: Moving Beyond Traditional Testing

Let's be honest; traditional tests have their place, but in a world where AI can ace multiple choice quizzes and generate flawless essays, we need to think differently about how we measure student learning.[35, 37] Performance-based assessments offer a powerful solution, allowing us to evaluate what students can actually do with their knowledge, not just what they can memorize or what AI can generate for them.

Think about it this way: Would you rather hire a chef who can perfectly recite recipes or one who can actually create delicious meals? Would you trust a mechanic who aced a written test about engines but has never fixed a car? Real-world success requires hands-on skills, creative problem-solving, and the ability to apply knowledge in authentic situations. This is exactly what performance-based assessments measure.

Performance-based assessments require students to demonstrate their understanding by completing complex, authentic tasks; such as conducting investigations, creating products, or solving real-world problems.[33, 35] Instead of selecting from multiple-choice options or writing formulaic essays, students might design an experiment to test water quality in local streams, develop a business plan for a community need, or create a documentary about a historical event using primary sources.

What makes these assessments particularly valuable in our AI-enhanced world is their emphasis on process, not just product.[35] When students document their thinking, defend their choices, and reflect on their learning journey, they create evidence of understanding that can't be easily replicated by AI tools. This approach also aligns perfectly with how learning happens in the real world: through trial, error, reflection, and revision.

Here are some key principles for designing effective performance-based assessments:

- Make it authentic: Connect assignments to real-world challenges and contexts that matter to your students[36, 37]
- Focus on process: Require documentation of thinking, research, and decision-making through portfolios or process journals[35]
- Build in reflection: Include opportunities for students to explain their choices and evaluate their own learning
- Use clear criteria: Develop detailed rubrics that emphasize both process and product[35, 37]
- Incorporate collaboration: Include elements that require real-time interaction and teamwork

The beauty of performance-based assessment is that it naturally resists AI shortcuts while deepening student engagement.[34, 35] When students investigate local environmental issues, conduct original research, or create solutions to community problems, they're not just demonstrating knowledge; they're applying it in ways that matter.

One particularly effective approach is to structure assessments around what assessment experts call "transfer tasks," challenges that require students to apply their learning in new contexts.[35, 37] For example, rather than just asking students to analyze a historical event, have them connect that event to current issues in their community and propose solutions based on historical lessons learned. This kind of task requires a deep understanding that goes beyond what AI can generate.

Remember, the goal isn't to make assignments "AI-proof"—that's probably impossible and misses the point. Instead, we want to create assessments that make AI irrelevant because the real value lies in the student's unique perspective, process, and growth.[35] When designed well, performance-based assessments don't just measure learning; they deepen it.[33, 36]

As you begin to incorporate more performance-based assessments into your teaching, start small. Choose one unit or concept where you can replace a traditional test with a performance task. Pay attention to how your students engage with the work and how it affects their learning. You might be surprised by how much more you learn about what your students actually know and can do.

In our next section, we'll explore specific strategies for creating authentic project-based evaluations that both challenge students and maintain academic integrity in an AI-enhanced world. But for now, remember: When we shift our focus from what students can remember to what they can do with their knowledge, we create assessment experiences that are both more meaningful and more resistant to AI shortcuts.[33, 35, 36]

Creating Authentic Project-Based Evaluations That Resist AI Shortcuts

Project-based learning has always been a powerful teaching tool, but in the age of AI, it's becoming our secret weapon for creating meaningful, cheat-resistant assessments. When students engage in well-designed projects that connect to their lives and communities, they're not just demonstrating knowledge; they're creating something uniquely their own that AI simply can't replicate.[38, 39]

Let's start with a fundamental truth: AI excels at generating generic responses to standard prompts, but it struggles with tasks requiring personal connection, real-world application, and documented process work.[38, 39] This is where authentic project-based evaluations shine. They ask students to apply their learning to genuine challenges, document their thinking process, and create solutions that matter to them and their communities.[40]

Here are key strategies for designing project-based assessments that naturally resist AI shortcuts while deepening student engagement:

- Embed local context and personal relevance: Have students investigate issues in their own community or connect course content to their lived experiences[40, 41]

- Require process documentation: Ask for research notes, drafts, and reflection logs that reveal student thinking over time[38, 40]
- Include collaborative elements: Build in peer feedback sessions and group work that demand real-time interaction[38, 40]
- Add oral components: Incorporate presentations or project defenses where students explain their thinking[39, 40, 41]
- Focus on iteration: Ask students to document multiple drafts and explain their revision decisions[38, 40]

One particularly effective approach is what assessment experts call the "Process-Product Assessment Approach." This method, successfully piloted at Birzeit University, requires students to document every step of their project work, including any AI tool usage. The results showed that students who initially tried to rely solely on AI-generated content struggled when asked to provide drafts and explain their process, leading them to engage more deeply with the material.[38]

When designing project-based assessments, think about creating what we call "layered challenges," tasks that build upon each other and require students to demonstrate understanding in multiple ways. For example, rather than just asking students to research environmental issues, have them:

- Investigate a specific environmental challenge in their local community[40]
- Interview stakeholders and gather first-hand data[40]
- Analyze their findings and propose realistic solutions[40, 41]
- Present their work to community members[40, 41]
- Document their process and reflect on their learning[38, 40]

This layered approach makes AI shortcuts less feasible while creating more meaningful learning experiences. Each layer requires original thinking, personal connection, and real-world application; elements that AI tools can't easily replicate.[39, 40, 41]

To support this kind of authentic assessment, we need to update our rubrics to emphasize process, originality, and ethical AI use.[38] Clear criteria help students understand expectations while making evaluation more manageable for us. Consider including categories like:

- Evidence of research process and source evaluation[38, 40]
- Documentation of project development and iteration[38, 40]
- Quality of real-world connections and applications[40, 41]
- Depth of personal reflection and critical thinking[39, 40]
- Appropriate and documented use of AI tools (when relevant)[38, 40]

Remember, the goal isn't to make assignments completely AI-proof; that's probably impossible and misses the point. Instead, we want to create projects where AI might be a useful tool but can't replace the essential human elements of learning, thinking, and creating.[38, 40]

As you begin implementing these strategies, start small. Choose one unit where you can transform a traditional assessment into a project-based evaluation. Pay attention to how your students engage with the work and how it affects their learning. You might be surprised by the depth of thinking and originality that emerges when students tackle real challenges that matter to them.[40, 41]

In the end, authentic project-based assessments do more than just resist AI shortcuts; they help prepare our students for a future where the ability to think critically, solve real problems, and work collaboratively will be more valuable than ever. When we design these kinds of meaningful evaluations, we're not just assessing learning; we're creating opportunities for genuine growth and engagement.[40, 41]

Building Portfolio Assessment Systems That Showcase Original Thinking

In the evolving landscape of AI and education, portfolio assessment has emerged as one of our most powerful tools for showcasing genuine student learning.[42, 3] Unlike traditional assignments that might be vulnerable to AI generation, well-designed portfolios capture the journey of learning; the messy middle, the breakthrough moments, and the authentic growth that no AI can easily replicate.[3]

Let's be clear: the goal of portfolio assessment isn't to make cheating impossible; it's to make original thinking irresistible.[43, 3] When students collect and curate evidence of their learning over time, they're not just completing assignments; they're telling their unique story of growth and understanding.[3]

Here are the essential elements of an effective portfolio system that naturally showcases original thinking:[3]

- Process documentation: Include drafts, reflections, and feedback cycles that show how ideas evolve
- Contextualized artifacts: Incorporate personal experiences and local connections that AI can't fabricate

- Multi-modal evidence: Combine written work with videos, audio reflections, and visual elements
- Regular self-reflection: Ask students to explain their thinking process and learning journey
- Real-time components: Include presentations or discussions that demonstrate genuine understanding

One of the most powerful aspects of portfolio assessment is its emphasis on metacognitive reflection.[3] When students regularly document not just what they learned but how they learned it, they create a record of thinking that's uniquely their own. This kind of deep reflection is something that AI tools simply cannot generate convincingly.

To implement an effective portfolio system, start with clear guidelines about what constitutes evidence of learning.[3] Your rubrics should emphasize original thinking, personal connection, and growth over time. Consider including categories that evaluate how students:

- Connect course concepts to their personal experiences
- Document their research and thinking process
- Respond to and incorporate feedback
- Reflect on their learning and growth
- Demonstrate understanding through multiple formats

The beauty of portfolio assessment lies in its flexibility.[3] Students can showcase their learning through various means: written analyses, video presentations, annotated images, or audio reflections. This multi-modal approach not only makes AI replication more difficult but also allows students to play to their strengths while developing new skills.

When designing your portfolio system, transparency is key.[43, 3] Be clear with students about why you're using portfolios and how they benefit learning. Frame AI not as an enemy to be outsmarted, but as a tool that can support the portfolio process; for example, using AI to help brainstorm reflection questions or organize portfolio elements.

Remember to build in regular checkpoints and feedback opportunities.[3] These moments of interaction help students stay on track while creating a documented trajectory of growth that would be nearly impossible for AI to fabricate retroactively. Consider implementing portfolio conferences where students discuss their work and thinking process in real-time.

To make your portfolio system more manageable, start small.[3] Choose one unit or concept where you'll pilot the approach. Pay attention to how students engage with the process and adjust your system based on what you learn. You might be surprised by how naturally students embrace the opportunity to showcase their original thinking when given the right structure and support.

As you develop your portfolio system, keep equity and accessibility in mind.[3] Ensure all students have the tools and support they need to succeed. This might mean providing options for different types of evidence or scaffolding the skills needed for effective reflection and documentation.

The most successful portfolio systems create what assessment experts call a "rich picture" of student learning; one that captures not just what students know, but how they think, create, and grow.[3] When we design portfolio assessments this way, we're not just evaluating learning; we're fostering the kind of deep engagement and original thinking that will serve our students well in an AI-enhanced world.

Remember, the goal isn't perfection; it's progress. Start with what feels manageable, learn from what works (and what doesn't), and adjust as needed. Your portfolio system will evolve just as your students do, becoming more refined and effective over time.

Let's focus on building a foundation that celebrates and encourages original thinking. After all, that's what great teaching has always been about. As we wrap up our exploration of assessment in the AI age, let's pause to reflect on the journey we've taken together. We started with Noah's story of transformation; how he turned a crisis of AI-generated essays into an opportunity to deepen student learning through his Living Portfolio system. His experience reminds us that meaningful assessment isn't about outsmarting technology; it's about inspiring authentic engagement and genuine learning.

Through our discussion of performance-based assessments, authentic projects, and portfolio systems, we've discovered that the most effective evaluations in an AI-enhanced world share common elements: they emphasize process over product, require personal connection, and demand evidence of thinking over time. These aren't just strategies to prevent AI shortcuts; they're approaches that enhance learning and prepare students for real-world challenges.

But perhaps the most important lesson is this: AI isn't making assessment obsolete; it's pushing us to be more intentional about what we measure and why. When we design assessments that require students to document their thinking, connect learning to their lives, and demonstrate understanding in multiple ways, we're not just creating AI-resistant assignments; we're creating meaningful learning experiences.

As you begin implementing these strategies in your own classroom, remember to start small. Choose one unit where you can experiment with performance-based assessment. Try incorporating process documentation into your existing projects. Begin building a simple portfolio system. The goal isn't to revolutionize everything overnight; it's to evolve our assessment practices thoughtfully and sustainably.

And yes, there will be challenges. Students might resist the deeper thinking required by these new approaches. You'll likely need to refine your rubrics and adjust your expectations. But remember: every step toward more authentic assessment is a step toward better learning.

Before we move on, take a moment to consider your next steps. What's one assessment you could transform using the strategies we've discussed? How might you incorporate more process documentation into your existing assignments? What would a simple portfolio system look like in your classroom?

The future of assessment isn't about finding the perfect AI-proof assignment; it's about creating evaluations that matter, that challenge students to think deeply, and that showcase their unique voices and understanding. When we do that, we're not just assessing learning; we're inspiring it.

In our next chapter, we'll explore how to build essential future-ready skills across the curriculum, ensuring our students are prepared for an AI-enhanced world. But for now, trust that you have the tools and strategies to create assessments that both resist AI shortcuts and deepen student learning. After all, that's what great teaching has always been about.

Chapter 7:

Building Future-Ready Skills: AI Literacy Across the Curriculum

In today's rapidly evolving educational landscape, AI literacy isn't just another tech skill; it's becoming as fundamental as reading and writing for our students' future success. As we prepare our students for careers that may not even exist yet, we need to weave AI literacy naturally into our existing curriculum rather than treating it as a separate subject. In fact, every subject area presents unique opportunities for building these essential future-ready skills. Whether we're teaching science, history, literature, or math, the integration of AI literacy can transform how students engage with content while preparing them for an increasingly AI-driven world.

I've seen this transformation firsthand across disciplines. Math teachers using AI to help students understand complex problem-solving processes. History classes leveraging AI tools to analyze primary sources in new ways. Science labs incorporating AI data analysis to enhance student research capabilities. The key isn't adding AI as another subject to teach; it's weaving it naturally into what we already do best.

Zara's story perfectly illustrates this integrated approach. As a science teacher at a diverse urban high school, she noticed her students struggling to understand both the potential and limitations of AI in scientific research. She developed what she called the "AI Investigation Lab," where students used AI tools to analyze real environmental data from their local community. The project required students to compare AI-generated analysis with traditional scientific methods, teaching them when to trust AI insights and when to question them. In one memorable session, students discovered that an AI model had missed crucial local context about a nearby creek's pollution levels because it hadn't been trained on regional environmental factors. This led to a powerful discussion about the importance of human expertise and local knowledge in scientific research. Through this hands-on experience, Zara's students learned not just about environmental science but also about AI's role in modern scientific inquiry. By the end of the semester, her students had developed a nuanced understanding of how to use AI as a tool while maintaining their critical thinking skills and scientific rigor. The project became a model for other departments, showing how AI literacy could be meaningfully integrated into any subject area.

This chapter will explore practical strategies for embedding AI literacy across the curriculum, helping students develop the critical evaluation skills they need while deepening their understanding of core subject matter. We'll examine how different disciplines can naturally incorporate AI awareness and skills, turning our students from passive consumers of AI technology into informed, ethical users and creators.

Remember, we're not just teaching students how to use AI tools; we're helping them develop the discernment and wisdom to know when and how to use them effectively. This is about preparing them for a future where AI literacy is as fundamental as reading and writing, while ensuring they maintain their unique human capabilities for critical thinking, creativity, and ethical judgment.

Cross-Disciplinary AI Integration: Embedding AI Literacy in Core Subjects

Let's explore how AI literacy can be woven seamlessly into every subject area, creating rich learning experiences that prepare students for their AI-enhanced future.[1, 2] Think of AI literacy like a thread that strengthens the fabric of our teaching; it's not about adding another subject to our already packed curriculum, but about enhancing what we already do well.

In mathematics, AI integration might look like students using machine learning tools to analyze real-world data sets, helping them understand both statistical concepts and AI's role in data analysis.[44, 2] For instance, when teaching probability, students can examine how AI makes predictions and why those predictions aren't always accurate. This dual-purpose learning helps students grasp both mathematical concepts and AI's capabilities and limitations.

Science classes offer natural opportunities for AI integration. Students can use AI tools to analyze experimental data, model complex systems, or predict outcomes.[2] But more importantly, they learn to question AI's conclusions, understanding when human expertise and local context matter most. For example, when studying climate change, students might compare AI climate models with actual local weather patterns, learning both about meteorology and the importance of training data in AI systems.

In social studies, AI literacy takes on a different dimension. Students can explore how algorithms influence social media, election campaigns, and economic systems.[44, 1] They might analyze AI-generated news articles alongside human-written ones, developing critical media literacy skills while learning about current events. These exercises help students understand both the subject matter and the broader implications of AI in society.

Language arts classes provide particularly rich opportunities for AI integration. Students can explore AI as a writing tool while developing critical thinking about its output.[44, 1] They might use AI to generate initial ideas for essays, but then learn to evaluate, refine, and transform those ideas through their own analytical lens. This approach teaches both writing skills and responsible AI use.[44, 3]

The key to successful cross-disciplinary AI integration lies in maintaining a balance. We want students to understand AI's capabilities without becoming overly dependent on them.[44, 2] Here are some practical strategies for embedding AI literacy across subjects:

- Start with low-stakes activities that allow students to experiment with AI tools while focusing on subject-specific learning objectives
- Include regular discussions about AI's role, limitations, and ethical considerations within your subject area[44]
- Design assignments that require students to evaluate and critique AI-generated content rather than simply consuming it[44]
- Create opportunities for students to compare AI and human approaches to problem-solving in your discipline.[2]

Remember, the goal isn't to turn every class into a computer science course. Instead, we're preparing students to be informed, critical users of AI technology while deepening their understanding of our core subjects.[1, 2] This integrated approach helps students see AI not as a mysterious black box, but as a tool they can understand, evaluate, and use responsibly.

When introducing AI concepts in your subject area, start small. You might begin with simple demonstrations of how AI tools can support learning in your discipline.[2] As students become more comfortable, gradually introduce more complex applications and critical discussions. The key is to make these connections feel natural and relevant to your subject matter.

Most importantly, maintain focus on your core subject objectives. AI literacy should enhance, not overshadow, the fundamental skills and knowledge we're teaching.[44, 2] When done well, this integration helps students see the real-world relevance of their studies while developing essential future-ready skills.

Remember, you don't need to be an AI expert to integrate these concepts into your teaching. Start with what you know about your subject area and gradually explore how AI intersects with it.[1] Your subject expertise, combined with a willingness to learn alongside your students, is the perfect foundation for this important work.

Building Critical AI Evaluation Skills: From Consumer to Creator

Moving from passive AI consumption to active evaluation and creation is one of the most crucial shifts we can help our students make. Think about it: our students are already immersed in AI-generated content, from their social media feeds to their Google search results. But how many of them can actually recognize when they're interacting with AI, let alone evaluate its reliability?

Let's start with a fundamental truth: critical AI evaluation isn't just about spotting AI-generated text or images. It's about developing a deeper understanding of how AI systems work, their limitations, and their potential impacts on society. This understanding forms the bridge between being a passive consumer and becoming an informed creator.

Here are the essential skills our students need to develop:

- Technical Literacy: Understanding basic AI concepts and how algorithms make decisions
- Ethical Awareness: Recognizing bias, fairness issues, and societal impacts
- Critical Analysis: Evaluating AI outputs for accuracy, reliability, and appropriateness
- Creative Application: Using AI tools thoughtfully and responsibly

One effective approach is to start with familiar territory. When teaching research skills, we can guide students to ask critical questions about AI-generated content: Where did the training data come from? What biases might be present? How can we verify this information? These questions build on traditional media literacy skills while addressing the unique challenges of AI.

Research from Long and Magerko (2020) suggests that effective AI literacy requires hands-on experience combined with critical reflection. This means creating opportunities for students to both use and evaluate AI tools in meaningful contexts. For instance, when students use AI writing assistants, we can guide them to analyze the suggestions they receive: Why did the AI make these recommendations? What assumptions might it be making? What cultural or contextual factors might it be missing?

The transition from consumer to creator doesn't happen overnight. Dr. Cynthia Breazeal, Director of MIT's Personal Robots Group, emphasizes that "AI literacy is not just about knowing how to code or use AI tools, but about understanding how AI shapes our society and being equipped to critically engage with it." This perspective reminds us that our goal isn't to turn every student into an AI programmer, but rather to develop informed digital citizens.

Here are some practical strategies for building these skills:

- Start with comparison exercises: Have students analyze both AI-generated and human-written texts on the same topic
- Incorporate ethical discussions: Use real-world cases like the COMPAS algorithm controversy to explore bias and fairness
- Encourage experimentation: Let students test different AI tools and document their observations

- Focus on reflection: Have students maintain journals about their AI interactions and insights

Remember, we're not just teaching students to use tools; we're teaching them to think critically about those tools. This means helping them understand both the capabilities and limitations of AI systems. When students recognize that AI can make mistakes, show bias, or lack important context, they're better equipped to use these tools responsibly.

The University of Toronto case study, where undergraduate students audited a facial recognition tool and uncovered significant racial and gender bias, shows the power of teaching critical evaluation skills. These students moved beyond being passive consumers to become active investigators, contributing meaningful insights to the broader discussion of AI ethics.

As Dr. Mark Riedl from Georgia Tech notes, "We must prepare students to be not just users of AI, but also designers, critics, and citizens who can hold these systems accountable." This perfectly captures our goal: developing students who can thoughtfully evaluate, ethically use, and potentially help shape the AI systems that will increasingly influence their lives.

Remember, you don't need to be an AI expert to guide students in developing these critical skills. Start with what you know about teaching critical thinking and gradually incorporate AI-specific elements. The key is to maintain a balance between embracing AI's potential while fostering the human skills of analysis, evaluation, and ethical judgment that no AI can replace.

Developing Ethical AI Awareness: Responsible Technology Use Across Disciplines

As we navigate the AI revolution in education, one of our most crucial responsibilities is helping students develop an ethical compass for using these powerful tools. It's not enough to simply teach the mechanics of AI; we need to foster a deep understanding of responsible technology use that spans every subject area.[1,2,3]

Think of ethical AI awareness as a lens through which students view their interactions with technology. Just as we teach digital citizenship for social media and internet use, we must now expand those conversations to include AI. This isn't about adding another item to our already full plates; it's about weaving ethical considerations naturally into our existing lessons.[1,2]

One effective approach is to incorporate regular reflective discussions about AI use across different subjects. In science classes, students might consider the implications of AI-generated research analysis. In history, they could explore how AI algorithms might interpret historical events differently from human historians. In literature, discussions might center on the authenticity of AI-generated creative writing.[2]

Here are some key principles to embed across disciplines:

- Transparency: Encourage students to openly acknowledge when and how they use AI tools[1]
- Critical evaluation: Teach students to question AI outputs and recognize potential biases

- Equity awareness: Discuss how AI access and impacts vary across different communities[1]
- Responsible creation: Guide students in using AI as a tool while maintaining their unique voice

The goal isn't to make every class a lesson in AI ethics. Instead, we want to help students develop an intuitive understanding of responsible AI use that becomes second nature. This means creating opportunities for ethical discussions that arise naturally from subject-matter content.[1, 2]

For example, when teaching research methods, we can guide students to ask critical questions about AI-generated content: Where did the training data come from? What biases might be present? How can we verify this information? These questions build on traditional critical thinking skills while addressing the unique challenges of AI.[1, 2]

One particularly effective strategy is to incorporate scenario-based learning across disciplines. Present students with real-world ethical dilemmas involving AI use and encourage them to think through the implications. This approach helps make abstract concepts concrete and relevant to their daily lives.[2]

Remember, developing ethical AI awareness isn't just about preventing misuse; it's about empowering students to become responsible digital citizens who understand both the potential and limitations of AI technology. By embedding these discussions across disciplines, we help students build a framework for ethical decision-making that will serve them well beyond the classroom.[1, 2, 3]

Here are some practical ways to integrate ethical AI awareness in different subjects:

- Mathematics: Explore algorithmic bias and its real-world impacts
- Social Studies: Analyze how AI influences social systems and policy decisions
- Language Arts: Discuss authorship, originality, and the role of AI in creative expression[24]
- Science: Examine the ethical implications of AI in research and data analysis

The key is maintaining a balance between embracing AI's potential while fostering the human skills of ethical reasoning and critical judgment. We want our students to see AI not as a shortcut, but as a tool that requires thoughtful, responsible use.[2, 3]

As educators, we play a crucial role in shaping how the next generation will use AI. By making ethical awareness a natural part of our teaching across disciplines, we help students develop the moral compass they'll need to navigate an increasingly AI-driven world. Remember, you don't need to be an AI expert to guide these important conversations; you just need to be willing to explore these questions alongside your students.[1, 2] As we conclude our exploration of building future-ready skills and AI literacy across the curriculum, let's take a moment to reflect on the transformative potential we've uncovered. We've seen how AI literacy isn't just another checkbox on our endless to-do list; it's a fundamental shift in how we prepare students for their future while deepening their engagement with our core subjects.

Through our journey in this chapter, we've explored practical strategies for weaving AI awareness into every subject area. From Zara's innovative science investigations to creative applications in the humanities, we've seen how AI literacy can enhance rather than detract from our core teaching objectives. The key insight? AI literacy isn't an add-on; it's a lens that can sharpen our students' understanding of traditional subjects while preparing them for an AI-enhanced world.

Remember these essential takeaways as you begin integrating AI literacy into your own classroom:

- Start where you are comfortable: You don't need to transform your entire curriculum overnight
- Focus on critical thinking: Help students evaluate AI tools, not just use them
- Keep it relevant: Connect AI concepts to your subject area in meaningful ways
- Emphasize ethical awareness: Make responsible AI use a natural part of every discussion

As we move forward in our AI teaching journey, remember that you're not just teaching students how to use technology; you're helping them develop the wisdom to know when and how to use it effectively. Your expertise as an educator, combined with these new AI literacy strategies, creates a powerful foundation for student success.

Let's carry forward the understanding that AI literacy isn't about diminishing human capabilities; it's about enhancing them. When we help students become thoughtful consumers and creators of AI technology, we're preparing them not just for future careers, but for informed citizenship in an AI-enhanced world.

As you close this chapter and begin implementing these ideas in your classroom, remember that you don't need to have all the answers. Sometimes the most powerful learning happens when we explore and question alongside our students. Trust your instincts as an educator, start small, and build confidence gradually.

You've already taken the first step by engaging with these ideas. Now it's time to bring them into your classroom, one lesson at a time. Remember, every expert was once a beginner, and every innovation in education started with a teacher willing to try something new.

In our next chapter, we'll explore the ethical dimensions of AI in education more deeply, building on the foundation of AI literacy we've established here. But for now, take a moment to appreciate how far you've come in understanding how to integrate these essential future-ready skills across your curriculum. You're not just teaching subjects anymore; you're preparing students for a future where AI literacy is as fundamental as reading and writing.

You've got this, and your students will be better prepared for their AI-enhanced future because of your willingness to embrace these changes thoughtfully and intentionally.

Chapter 8:

Ethics and Integrity: Navigating AI's Gray Areas

Ethics isn't just a chapter in a textbook; it's the foundation that determines whether AI will enhance or undermine education in our classrooms. As I watched my students grapple with the temptations and possibilities of AI tools, I realized we needed more than just rules; we needed a new ethical framework that would guide both teachers and students through this technological transformation. As we delve into the ethical dimensions of AI in education, we're confronted with questions that challenge our fundamental beliefs about teaching, learning, and academic integrity. It's a landscape where traditional notions of originality, assessment, and student growth intersect with powerful new technological capabilities.

Willa's story resonates deeply with many of us. She stood before her senior English class, holding a stack of papers that had kept her awake for three nights straight. Half of her students had used AI to write their college application essays; not maliciously, but because they genuinely didn't understand why it was problematic. Instead of responding with anger, she decided to turn this into a teachable moment. She developed what she called the "Authenticity Project," where students examined their AI-generated essays alongside their genuine writing. Through guided discussions, students discovered how the AI essays, while technically proficient, lacked their unique voices and personal insights. The breakthrough came when one student admitted that his AI-generated essay about overcoming challenges felt hollow because it didn't reflect his real experiences. This led to powerful conversations about authenticity, personal growth, and the true purpose of writing. By the end of the project, every student had rewritten their essays, this time drawing from their own experiences and voices. The lesson went beyond just teaching about AI ethics; it helped students understand the value of their own authentic voices in a world increasingly mediated by technology.

Willa's experience highlights a crucial truth: in the rush to adapt to AI technology, we can't lose sight of the human elements that make education meaningful. The ethical challenges we face aren't just about preventing cheating; they're about preserving authenticity, fostering genuine learning, and helping students understand the value of their own thoughts and experiences.

In this chapter, we'll explore practical frameworks for navigating these ethical complexities. We'll examine strategies for establishing clear guidelines, teaching responsible AI use, and creating a classroom culture that values both technological innovation and academic integrity. Most importantly, we'll discuss how to help our students develop their own ethical compass in a world where the line between human and machine-generated work grows increasingly blurred.

Remember, our goal isn't to become AI police officers or to create an atmosphere of suspicion. Instead, we're aiming to build an environment where students understand and value authentic learning, where they see AI as a tool to enhance their capabilities rather than a shortcut to bypass genuine engagement with their education.

As we explore these challenges and solutions together, you'll discover that addressing ethical concerns around AI use doesn't have to be overwhelming. With the right approach, we can help our students navigate this new landscape while maintaining the integrity of their educational experience.

Developing an Ethical AI Framework: Guidelines for Classroom Use

Let's start with a fundamental truth: creating ethical guidelines for AI use isn't about restricting learning; it's about enhancing it. Think of an ethical framework as a well-designed classroom management plan. Just as clear expectations help students thrive, thoughtful AI guidelines create an environment where technology serves learning rather than undermines it.

The foundation of any effective AI framework rests on several key principles that should guide our decisions. First and foremost is beneficence; ensuring that AI truly benefits all learners.[46] This means carefully evaluating each AI tool and practice to confirm it promotes student growth and well-being. We also need to prioritize fairness and justice, making sure our AI implementations don't inadvertently disadvantage any student groups.[46, 47]

Let's break this down into practical guidelines you can implement in your classroom:

- Transparency First: Be open with students about when and how AI tools are being used in your classroom.[46, 48] This builds trust and models digital citizenship.
- Clear Boundaries: Establish specific guidelines for when AI use is appropriate and when it isn't.[46, 48] For example, AI might be allowed for brainstorming but not for final drafts.
- Privacy Protection: Ensure any AI tools you're using have strong data protection measures.[45, 46] Remember, student privacy isn't optional; it's essential.
- Regular Assessment: Monitor how AI tools impact learning outcomes and be ready to adjust your approach based on what you observe,[45, 46]

One of the most crucial aspects of an ethical framework is promoting student autonomy.[46, 47] This means teaching students to make informed choices about AI use rather than simply imposing restrictions. When students understand the 'why' behind ethical guidelines, they're more likely to make responsible choices independently.

Accountability is another cornerstone of ethical AI use.[46, 45] This means being clear about who's responsible for AI-assisted work and establishing consequences that focus on learning rather than punishment. For instance, if a student uses AI inappropriately, the response should include reflection and education rather than just penalties.

Let's consider how this might look in practice. When introducing a new AI tool in your classroom, start with these questions:

- How will this tool enhance learning for all students?
- What safeguards are in place to protect student privacy and data?
- How can we ensure fair access and prevent bias?
- What boundaries need to be established for appropriate use?

Remember, developing an ethical framework isn't a one-time task; it's an ongoing process that should evolve with technology and student needs. The goal is to create guidelines that protect academic integrity while embracing the potential of AI to enhance learning.

One effective approach is to involve students in developing these guidelines.[47, 48] This not only helps them understand the importance of ethical AI use but also gives them ownership in the process. Ask them to consider scenarios where AI might help or hinder learning, and use their insights to refine your framework.

As you implement your framework, communication is key. Make sure all stakeholders, students, parents, and colleagues understand your guidelines and the reasoning behind them.[47] This transparency helps build support for your approach and ensures everyone is working toward the same goals.

Remember to regularly assess and adjust your framework.[45, 46] What works today might need refinement tomorrow as AI technology evolves. Stay informed about new developments in educational AI and be ready to update your guidelines accordingly.

Finally, don't forget to document your framework and share it with colleagues. Your experience can help other teachers develop their own ethical guidelines, creating a broader culture of responsible AI use in education.

The key to success is finding the right balance; between innovation and integrity, between guidance and autonomy, between embracing new tools and protecting educational values. With thoughtful planning and clear guidelines, AI can become a powerful ally in your teaching practice while maintaining the highest ethical standards.

Teaching Digital Ethics: Moving Beyond "Don't Cheat" to "Why Integrity Matters"

Moving beyond "don't cheat" requires a fundamental shift in how we approach digital ethics with our students.[1, 2, 3] In an AI-powered world, simply creating rules and consequences isn't enough; we need to help students understand the deeper value of academic integrity and develop their own ethical compass for navigating these new tools.[3]

The traditional approach of focusing solely on preventing cheating often backfires.[3] When we lead with prohibitions and threats, we miss the opportunity to engage students in meaningful discussions about why original thinking matters. Instead, we need to help students see integrity as an essential part of their learning journey, not just a set of rules to follow.[1, 3]

Let's explore some practical strategies for fostering genuine ethical understanding:

- Start with the "Why": Help students understand how original thinking contributes to their learning and growth

- Create opportunities for ethical decision-making practice through real-world scenarios
- Encourage transparency about AI use rather than treating it as something to hide[1]
- Focus on building intrinsic motivation rather than relying on external consequences[3]

One of the most powerful ways to teach digital ethics is through guided reflection and discussion.[2, 3] When students encounter ethical dilemmas involving AI, whether it's using a chatbot for brainstorming or an AI writing assistant for editing, encourage them to think through their choices carefully. Ask questions like: How does this tool support or potentially limit your learning? What's the difference between collaboration and dependence?

Research shows that students are more likely to make ethical choices when they understand the reasoning behind guidelines rather than just following rules.[3] By helping students see how integrity connects to their own goals and values, we can foster a more genuine commitment to ethical behavior.

A key part of this approach involves reframing how we talk about AI tools.[1, 2] Instead of positioning them as potential cheating devices, we can discuss them as powerful resources that require responsible use. This shifts the conversation from "what's not allowed" to "how can we use these tools ethically to enhance learning?"

To make this concrete, consider implementing these classroom practices:

- Regular class discussions about real-world AI ethics scenarios[2]
- Student-led development of classroom AI use guidelines
- Reflection journals where students document their decision-making around AI use
- Clear protocols for when and how to cite AI assistance[1]

Remember, our goal isn't to make students fear AI or feel guilty about using it. Instead, we want to help them develop the judgment and ethical awareness to use these tools responsibly.[2, 3] This means creating an environment where students feel comfortable asking questions and discussing challenges openly.

One effective approach is to use case studies that highlight the nuances of digital ethics.[1, 2] For example, you might discuss scenarios where AI use falls into gray areas: Is it appropriate to use AI for generating initial ideas? For checking grammar? For restructuring paragraphs? These discussions help students develop critical thinking skills about ethical technology use.

It's also crucial to address the broader implications of academic integrity.[1, 3] Help students understand that integrity isn't just about following school rules; it's about developing habits that will serve them in their future careers and lives. When students see the connection between classroom integrity and real-world success, they're more likely to take ownership of their ethical choices.

To support this understanding, consider incorporating these elements into your teaching:

- Examples of how integrity matters in various professions

- Discussions about the role of original thinking in innovation
- Exploration of how AI can support (rather than replace) human creativity.[1, 2]
- Clear guidelines for appropriate AI use in different contexts

Remember that teaching digital ethics is an ongoing process, not a one-time lesson.[2] As AI tools evolve, so too must our discussions about ethical use. Stay current with developments in educational AI and be prepared to adjust your approach as new challenges and opportunities arise.

By moving beyond simple prohibitions to deeper discussions about why integrity matters, we can help our students become not just ethical users of AI, but thoughtful digital citizens who understand the value of their own original thinking.[1, 2, 3] This approach not only promotes academic integrity but also prepares students for a future where ethical AI use will be an essential skill.

Creating a Culture of AI Responsibility: Policies and Practices That Work

Building a culture of AI responsibility isn't about creating a list of rules; it's about fostering an environment where ethical AI use becomes as natural as raising your hand before speaking. This transformation requires intentional effort, clear communication, and consistent modeling of responsible practices.[49, 51]

Let's start with a fundamental truth: effective AI policies grow from your institution's core values and mission. They shouldn't be generic documents copied from other schools or hastily assembled responses to challenges.[51] Instead, they should reflect your school's unique culture while incorporating essential ethical principles like beneficence, justice, and respect for student autonomy.[46, 49]

Here are key elements for building a strong foundation of AI responsibility:

- Mission Alignment: Ensure AI policies reflect your school's core values and educational goals[51]
- Stakeholder Engagement: Involve teachers, students, and parents in policy development[51]
- Clear Communication: Define roles, limitations, and expectations for AI use[50, 51]
- Regular Review: Create mechanisms to evaluate and update policies as technology evolves[51]

One of the most powerful ways to promote responsible AI use is through transparent communication. When students understand not just what's allowed but why certain guidelines exist, they're more likely to make ethical choices independently. This means having open discussions about how AI tools work, what data they collect, and how decisions are made.[50]

Professional development plays a crucial role in building this culture. Teachers need opportunities to explore ethical AI use through practical frameworks and real-world scenarios.[49] Consider establishing Professional Learning Communities (PLCs) focused on AI ethics, where educators can share experiences, discuss challenges, and develop best practices together.[49]

Here's what effective professional development for AI responsibility might include:

- Hands-on workshops exploring ethical decision-making frameworks[49]
- Regular discussions of real-world AI scenarios and solutions[51]
- Collaborative development of classroom guidelines[49]
- Ongoing support for implementing AI tools responsibly[51]

Remember, we're not aiming for perfect compliance with a rigid set of rules. Instead, we're working to develop what I call 'ethical fluency,' the ability to navigate AI-related decisions thoughtfully and responsibly. This means helping students understand the broader implications of their choices and teaching them to think critically about when and how to use AI tools.[49]

A balanced approach is key. Rather than taking extreme positions, either banning AI entirely or embracing it without question, we need to model thoughtful integration that enhances learning while maintaining academic integrity.[49] This might mean showing students how to use AI for brainstorming while emphasizing the importance of original thinking in final work.

Here are practical strategies for promoting responsible AI use in your classroom:

- Create clear protocols for citing AI assistance[50]
- Develop rubrics that value both AI-enhanced and traditional work methods[50]
- Establish checkpoints for reviewing AI-assisted work[50]

- Build reflection opportunities into assignments[49]

One particularly effective approach is to blend AI tools with traditional pedagogies. This isn't about replacing proven teaching methods; it's about enhancing them with technology where appropriate.[50] For example, you might use AI to generate initial writing prompts but rely on peer review and teacher feedback for developing student voice and style.

Remember that building a culture of AI responsibility is an ongoing process. It requires regular assessment and adjustment as technology evolves and new challenges emerge.[51] Stay informed about developments in educational AI, but don't feel pressured to adopt every new tool or trend. Focus on what serves your students' learning needs while upholding academic integrity.[49]

Most importantly, approach this work with patience and persistence. Cultural change doesn't happen overnight, but with consistent effort and clear communication, we can create learning environments where responsible AI use becomes second nature.[51] Keep the focus on supporting student learning and growth, and let that guide your decisions about AI integration.

As you develop and refine your approach to AI responsibility, remember that you're not just creating rules; you're shaping how the next generation will think about and use these powerful tools.[49] That's both a significant responsibility and an incredible opportunity to prepare students for their AI-enhanced future. As we conclude our exploration of ethics and integrity in AI education, it's worth reflecting on how far we've come in this chapter. We've moved from viewing AI as a potential threat to understanding it as a powerful tool that, when used ethically, can enhance both teaching and learning. Through Willa's story and our examination of ethical frameworks, we've seen how thoughtful implementation of AI can actually strengthen academic integrity rather than compromise it.

The journey through this chapter has revealed several crucial insights. First, effective AI ethics isn't about creating more rules; it's about fostering understanding and developing sound judgment. Second, when we focus on teaching students why integrity matters rather than just telling them not to cheat, we create opportunities for deeper learning and genuine engagement. Finally, building a culture of AI responsibility requires consistent effort, clear communication, and a commitment to modeling ethical behavior.

As you return to your classroom, remember that you don't have to have all the answers figured out immediately. Start small with the framework we've discussed, adapt it to your specific context, and be willing to adjust as you learn what works best for your students. The goal isn't perfection; it's progress toward a classroom culture where ethical AI use becomes second nature.

Here are the key takeaways as you move forward:

- Focus on building understanding rather than just enforcing rules
- Create opportunities for students to practice ethical decision-making
- Stay flexible and adjust your approach as technology evolves
- Keep the emphasis on learning and growth rather than compliance

- Document what works and share your successes with colleagues

Remember that you're not just teaching students how to use AI tools; you're helping them develop the ethical framework they'll need to navigate an increasingly AI-driven world. Your role in this process is crucial, and the time you invest in developing these guidelines and practices will pay dividends in student learning and growth.

As we move into our next chapter on differentiation, keep in mind that the ethical principles we've discussed here will inform how we approach personalizing learning with AI. The foundation of trust and integrity we build now will make it easier to implement AI-powered differentiation strategies effectively and responsibly.

You've got this! Remember, ethical AI implementation isn't a destination; it's an ongoing journey of growth and adaptation. Stay curious, keep learning, and don't hesitate to revise your approach as you gain experience and confidence. Your commitment to ethical AI use is helping shape not just your classroom, but the future of education itself.

Chapter 9:

Differentiation Made Easy: Using AI for Personalized Learning

Differentiation has always been the holy grail of teaching; we know it's crucial, but achieving it for thirty different learners has felt like trying to solve a Rubik's Cube in the dark. But with AI as our assistant, we can finally turn the lights on and see all the patterns, possibilities, and pathways to reach every student in our classroom. As we delve into the transformative potential of AI for differentiated instruction, let's start with a story that illustrates both the challenges and possibilities that technology brings to personalized learning.

Harper walked into her classroom one morning, already dreading the challenge ahead. Her third-period class included students reading at five different grade levels, three English language learners, and several gifted students who finished their work at lightning speed. Traditional differentiation meant creating multiple versions of every assignment, a task that often kept her working until midnight. Desperate for a solution, she began experimenting with AI tools to help modify reading materials and create leveled assignments. She developed what she called the "Adaptive Learning Framework," using AI to generate different versions of texts while maintaining core learning objectives. The breakthrough came when she used AI to create a bank of scaffolded questions that could be quickly customized for different learning needs. Within weeks, her students were more engaged because they were working at their optimal challenge levels. One struggling reader, who usually sat silently during discussions, began actively participating because he could access the content in a way that made sense to him. By the end of the semester, Harper had cut her planning time by 60% while actually providing more personalized support to her students. Her approach became a model for other teachers in her school, showing how AI could make true differentiation both practical and sustainable.

Harper's experience reflects a common struggle in modern classrooms: the challenge of meeting diverse learning needs while maintaining our sanity and work-life balance. The promise of differentiated instruction has long been shadowed by the practical limitations of time, resources, and energy. But AI is changing this equation, offering tools that can help us scale our expertise and provide more personalized learning experiences without doubling our workload.

In this chapter, we'll explore practical strategies for using AI to support differentiation across various learning styles, ability levels, and student needs. We'll examine how to create adaptive content that maintains rigor while providing appropriate scaffolding, and we'll look at ways to use AI tools to track and respond to student progress more efficiently. Most importantly, we'll focus on sustainable practices that you can implement without feeling overwhelmed.

The goal isn't to replace your professional judgment with algorithms, but to amplify your ability to reach every student in your classroom. Whether you're supporting struggling readers, challenging advanced learners, or accommodating different learning styles, AI can help make differentiation more manageable and effective. Let's explore how to make this technology work for you and your students.

AI-Powered Learning Profiles: Understanding and Responding to Student Needs

Understanding our students has always been at the heart of effective teaching, but keeping track of thirty different learning journeys can feel like juggling while riding a unicycle. AI-powered learning profiles are changing this dynamic, offering us a way to gather, analyze, and act on student data that goes beyond traditional assessment methods.[2, 52]

Think of AI learning profiles as dynamic digital portraits that capture not just what students know, but how they learn best.[2] These profiles continuously update as students interact with digital learning tools, complete assignments, and engage in classroom activities.[2] The AI analyzes patterns in everything from reading speeds to problem-solving approaches, helping us spot trends we might miss in the daily classroom rush.[52]

But let's be clear; these aren't just fancy spreadsheets. Modern AI learning profiles can identify when a student's engagement patterns shift, flag potential learning challenges before they become obstacles, and suggest personalized learning strategies based on each student's unique needs.[2, 10] For example, the AI might notice that a student consistently struggles with specific types of math problems but excels when the same concepts are presented visually, allowing us to adjust our teaching approach accordingly.[2, 10]

The real power of AI learning profiles lies in their ability to help us make data-driven decisions without drowning in spreadsheets.[10, 52] Instead of spending hours analyzing assessment data, we can focus on what matters most, using these insights to support our students.[10] The AI can suggest grouping strategies for collaborative work, recommend specific interventions for struggling learners, and identify opportunities for enrichment for students who need additional challenges.[2, 10]

However, it's crucial to remember that AI learning profiles are tools to enhance our professional judgment, not replace it.[10, 52] They should inform our decisions, not make them for us. As we implement these systems, we need to maintain a careful balance between leveraging technology and preserving student privacy.[2, 4] This means being transparent about data collection, ensuring compliance with privacy laws, and regularly auditing AI recommendations for potential bias.[4]

Here are some practical ways to start using AI learning profiles effectively:

- Begin with Clear Goals: Define what you want to learn about your students and how you'll use the insights.[2, 10]
- Start Small: Focus on one aspect of student learning first, like reading comprehension or math problem-solving[2]
- Involve Students: Share appropriate insights with students to help them understand their own learning patterns[10]
- Regular Review: Set aside time each week to review the AI's insights and plan interventions[2, 52]

The implementation of AI learning profiles isn't just about collecting data; it's about using that information to create more responsive, inclusive classrooms.[2, 4] When used thoughtfully, these tools can help us identify struggling students earlier, provide more targeted support, and ensure that every student has the opportunity to succeed.[52]

Remember that integrating AI learning profiles is a journey, not a destination.[2, 10] Start with small steps, celebrate the wins, and don't be afraid to adjust your approach based on what works best for your students. The goal isn't to create perfect profiles overnight but to gradually build a more complete understanding of each learner in your classroom.[2]

As we continue to explore the potential of AI in education, learning profiles represent one of the most promising tools for making differentiation more manageable and effective.[2, 10] They help us turn the abstract ideal of personalized learning into a practical reality, allowing us to support each student's unique learning journey while maintaining our sanity in the process.[10]

Creating Adaptive Content: Using AI to Modify Materials for Different Learners

One of the most powerful ways AI is transforming education is through its ability to help us modify and adapt learning materials for different students.[53, 54] Gone are the days of spending hours creating three different versions of the same worksheet; AI can now help us generate multiple variations of content while maintaining the core learning objectives.[53, 57]

Let's be honest: we've all had that moment of guilt when we couldn't provide properly leveled materials for every student in our classroom. Maybe it was that Shakespeare unit where your English language learners needed simplified text, your advanced readers craved deeper analysis, and your struggling readers needed additional scaffolding. Creating all those variations manually would take hours we simply don't have.

AI tools are changing this landscape dramatically. They can help us:

- Adjust reading levels while preserving key concepts and vocabulary
- Generate multiple versions of practice problems at different difficulty levels
- Create varied scaffolding supports for complex texts
- Develop differentiated writing prompts that maintain rigor while providing appropriate support.[53, 54, 55]

The key to using AI for content adaptation effectively lies in understanding what we want to preserve and what we're willing to modify. For instance, when adapting a complex text, we might want to maintain key vocabulary and central themes while simplifying sentence structure and providing additional context clues.[54]

Let's look at how this works in practice. When using AI to modify content, start by identifying your learning objectives and non-negotiables; the elements that must remain consistent across all versions. Then, specify the types of adaptations needed for different learners.[54, 55] For example, you might ask the AI to:

- Simplify language while retaining key terms
- Add visual supports or analogies
- Include more frequent comprehension checks
- Provide additional background information[53, 54]

However, it's crucial to remember that AI is an assistant, not a replacement for our professional judgment. While AI can generate different versions of content quickly, we need to review and refine these adaptations to ensure they truly meet our students' needs. Think of AI as your differentiation partner; it can handle the heavy lifting of initial content modification, but you bring the essential understanding of your students' specific needs and learning styles.[53, 57]

One particularly effective strategy is using AI to create what I call "layered content," materials that include built-in scaffolding that can be peeled away as students develop mastery. This might include:

- Embedded vocabulary support that can be toggled on or off
- Guided questions that become progressively more complex
- Optional background information that advanced learners can skip[54, 55]

The real power of AI-adapted content lies not just in its ability to modify materials but in how it can help us maintain high expectations while providing appropriate support. When done well, AI-assisted differentiation means every student can access challenging content and engage in meaningful learning.[54, 55]

Remember to regularly assess the effectiveness of your AI-modified materials. Are students engaging more deeply with the content? Are they showing better understanding? Are they moving toward independence? Use these insights to refine your approach and ensure that technology truly serves your teaching goals.[55, 56]

As with any teaching tool, the key is to start small and build confidence gradually. You might begin by using AI to modify a single reading passage or create differentiated writing prompts for one assignment. As you become more comfortable with the process, you can expand to more complex adaptations and broader implementation.[53, 54]

The goal isn't to create perfectly differentiated materials for every lesson; that's neither practical nor necessary. Instead, focus on using AI to make strategic adaptations that will have the biggest impact on your students' learning. With practice and thoughtful implementation, AI can help us create more inclusive, engaging, and effective learning experiences for all our students.[53, 54, 55, 56, 57]

Automated Differentiation Strategies: From Content to Assessment

Let's talk about one of the most exciting developments in education technology: the ability to automate differentiation strategies across both content delivery and assessment. If you're like most teachers, the phrase "differentiated instruction" probably triggers both enthusiasm and exhaustion; we know it's vital for student success, but the practical implementation has traditionally felt like trying to be in thirty places at once.[58, 59, 60]

The good news? AI is transforming this landscape in remarkable ways. According to recent studies, AI-powered differentiation tools have shown a 25% improvement in student grades, test scores, and engagement compared to traditional instruction methods.[59] But what does this mean for our daily teaching practice?

Let's break down how automated differentiation actually works in today's classroom. Think of AI as your differentiation assistant, capable of analyzing student performance patterns and automatically adjusting content and assessments in real-time.[58, 59] For instance, when a student consistently struggles with specific types of math problems but excels when concepts are presented visually, AI systems can automatically adapt future content to match this learning preference.[59, 60]

Here are some practical ways AI is revolutionizing differentiation:

- Real-time feedback systems that adjust question difficulty based on student responses[58, 59]
- Automatic translation and language support for English language learners[60]
- Dynamic content adaptation that maintains core learning objectives while adjusting complexity levels[58, 59]
- Culturally responsive material generation that reflects student backgrounds[60]

But let's be honest; implementing these tools effectively requires a thoughtful approach. Start small by identifying one aspect of your teaching where automated differentiation could make the biggest impact.[61] Maybe it's generating differentiated reading passages for your literature unit, or creating leveled math practice problems that automatically adjust to student performance.[58, 59]

One particularly powerful application is in assessment. AI can now help us create what I call "responsive assessments," tests and quizzes that automatically adjust their difficulty level based on student responses while maintaining alignment with curriculum standards.[59] This means every student is appropriately challenged, from those who need extra support to those ready for advanced content.

However, it's crucial to remember that AI is a tool to enhance our professional judgment, not replace it. When implementing automated differentiation strategies, consider these key principles:

- Always review AI-generated materials for accuracy and appropriateness
- Monitor student data privacy and ensure compliance with FERPA regulations
- Regularly assess the effectiveness of automated adaptations[59, 61]
- Maintain the human element in your teaching; technology should support, not supplant, your relationship with students

The real power of automated differentiation lies in its ability to help us scale our expertise. Instead of spending hours creating multiple versions of the same assignment, we can focus our energy on what matters most: meaningful interactions with our students and targeted interventions where they're needed most.[58, 59]

Remember those adaptive AI tutoring systems being used in Midwest high schools? They're showing us what's possible when we combine teacher expertise with AI capabilities.[59] Teachers report spending less time on administrative tasks and more time on meaningful student interactions, while students feel more supported and engaged in their learning journey.

As we implement these tools, it's essential to maintain clear goals and monitor progress.[61] Are students showing improved engagement? Is learning becoming more personalized and effective? Are we saving time while maintaining high standards? These questions should guide our use of automated differentiation tools.

The future of differentiation isn't about replacing teacher judgment; it's about amplifying our ability to meet each student where they are.[58, 59, 60] With AI as our partner, we can create truly inclusive classrooms where every student has the opportunity to succeed, without burning ourselves out in the process.

Remember, you don't need to implement everything at once. Start with one tool or strategy, get comfortable with it, and gradually expand your automated differentiation toolkit.[61] The goal isn't perfection; it's progress toward more personalized, efficient, and effective teaching for all our students. As we conclude our exploration of AI-powered differentiation, let's pause to reflect on how far we've come. From Harper's breakthrough with her Adaptive Learning Framework to the practical implementation of AI learning profiles and automated assessment strategies, we've seen how technology can transform the way we meet diverse student needs.

The journey to effective differentiation has always been challenging. We entered teaching with grand visions of reaching every student, only to find ourselves overwhelmed by the practical realities of creating multiple versions of every lesson, providing individualized feedback, and tracking thirty different learning journeys. AI isn't a magic solution to these challenges, but it is a powerful ally in making differentiation more manageable and effective.

Let's recap the key strategies we've explored:

- Using AI learning profiles to understand and respond to student needs more efficiently
- Creating adaptive content that maintains rigor while providing appropriate support
- Implementing automated differentiation strategies that scale our expertise without sacrificing quality

But perhaps the most important lesson isn't about the technology itself; it's about how these tools can help us reclaim time for what matters most: meaningful interactions with our students. When AI handles the heavy lifting of content modification and initial assessment analysis, we can focus on building relationships, providing targeted support, and celebrating student growth.

As you begin implementing these strategies in your own classroom, remember to start small. Choose one area where differentiation feels most challenging and experiment with AI support there. Maybe it's creating leveled reading passages for your literature unit, or developing scaffolded writing prompts for your next essay assignment. The goal isn't to revolutionize your entire teaching practice overnight;

it's to gradually build a more responsive, inclusive classroom where every student can thrive.

Remember that moment when we compared differentiation to solving a Rubik's Cube in the dark? With AI as our assistant, we're not just turning on the lights; we're gaining a partner who can help us see patterns, possibilities, and pathways we might have missed on our own. The future of differentiated instruction isn't about replacing teacher judgment with algorithms; it's about amplifying our ability to meet each student where they are while maintaining our sanity and work-life balance.

As we close this chapter, I want to acknowledge that adopting new technology can feel daunting. You might be wondering if you're ready for this shift, if you have the technical skills needed, or if your students will respond well to these changes. These concerns are natural and valid. But remember: you don't need to be a tech expert to use AI effectively. You just need to be what you already are: a dedicated teacher committed to helping every student succeed.

In the next chapter, we'll explore how to become an AI innovation champion in your school community, sharing your successes and supporting colleagues on their own journeys toward AI-enhanced teaching. But for now, take a moment to celebrate how far you've come. You're not just learning about new tools; you're part of a transformation that's making truly personalized learning possible for every student in your classroom.

You've got this, and your students will benefit from every small step you take toward more effective differentiation. Keep experimenting, keep learning, and most importantly, keep believing in the power of reaching every learner in your classroom; now with a little help from your AI teaching assistant.

Chapter 10:

Leading the AI Transformation: Becoming Your School's Innovation Champion

Leadership isn't just about having a vision; it's about helping others see the possibilities and feel confident enough to take that first step. As I discovered while helping my school navigate its AI transformation, becoming an innovation champion requires equal parts expertise, empathy, and strategic thinking. The journey to becoming an AI champion in your school isn't about being the most tech-savvy teacher or having all the answers; it's about being willing to experiment, learn, and share your discoveries with others. In my experience, the most effective AI leaders aren't necessarily those with computer science degrees; they're educators who understand both the potential and limitations of these tools in real classroom settings.

As we'll explore in this chapter, leading an AI transformation requires a delicate balance of technical knowledge, pedagogical wisdom, and interpersonal skills. You'll learn how to build support among colleagues, address common concerns, and create sustainable change that enhances teaching and learning across your school community.

Let me share a story about Skye, a teacher whose journey from AI experimenter to school innovation leader perfectly illustrates the transformative power of collaborative leadership. Skye never set out to become her school's AI champion; it happened organically after she started sharing her successful experiments with AI-enhanced writing instruction in department meetings. What began as casual conversations with curious colleagues evolved into informal lunch-and-learn sessions where she demonstrated how AI tools could streamline grading and improve student feedback.

The turning point came when her principal asked her to lead a professional development session on AI integration. Initially nervous about presenting to the entire faculty, Skye decided to focus on practical demonstrations rather than theoretical discussions. She showed her colleagues how she used AI to create differentiated writing prompts in real-time, generate personalized feedback templates, and design more engaging assignments. The response was overwhelming; teachers who had been skeptical about AI began asking for one-on-one guidance.

Within months, Skye had established a weekly AI learning circle where teachers could share challenges, celebrate successes, and support each other's growth. Her approach of leading with empathy, focusing on practical applications, and creating a safe space for experimentation transformed her school's attitude toward AI. By year's end, even the most tech-resistant teachers were exploring AI tools, and student engagement had noticeably improved across multiple subjects. Skye's journey from curious experimenter to respected innovation leader showed how one teacher's willingness to share and support others could catalyze meaningful change throughout an entire school community.

As we dive into the strategies and insights that can help you become your school's AI champion, remember that leadership is less about having all the answers and more about asking the right questions. It's about creating spaces where colleagues feel safe to experiment, fail, learn, and grow together. Whether you're just starting to explore AI in your classroom or you're ready to help others do the same, this chapter will provide you with the practical tools and confidence you need to lead your school's AI transformation.

Most importantly, you'll discover that becoming an AI champion isn't about pushing technology for technology's sake; it's about fostering a culture of innovation that puts student learning and teacher well-being at the center of every decision. Let's explore how you can take those first steps toward becoming the change agent your school needs in this exciting era of AI-enhanced education.

Building Teacher Buy-In: Creating a Supportive AI Learning Community

Creating a culture of AI innovation in your school isn't about forcing technology adoption; it's about nurturing a community where teachers feel supported, valued, and empowered to experiment. Think of it like starting a garden: you need the right conditions, patient cultivation, and a supportive environment for growth to flourish.

One of the most powerful ways to build teacher buy-in is through what I call the "Three C's": Connection, Confidence, and Collaboration. Let's explore how these elements work together to create a thriving AI learning community.

Connection means helping teachers see AI as a partner rather than a threat.[1] When introducing AI tools to your colleagues, start with their pain points. What tasks keep them up at night? Which responsibilities drain their energy? By showing how AI can address these real challenges, like providing quick feedback on student drafts or generating differentiated writing prompts, you help teachers connect AI's potential to their daily needs.

Confidence grows through hands-on experience and supportive mentorship.[2] Consider organizing informal "Tech and Talk" lunch sessions where teachers can experiment with AI tools in a low-stakes environment. Share your own learning journey, including the missteps and discoveries. Remember, every expert was once a beginner, and acknowledging this helps create psychological safety for learning.

Collaboration amplifies individual success into collective growth.[2] Create opportunities for teachers to share their AI experiments, both successful and unsuccessful. This could be through a dedicated Slack channel, regular department meetings, or a shared digital repository of AI-enhanced lesson plans and activities.

Here are some practical strategies for building your school's AI learning community:

- Start Small: Begin with a pilot group of interested teachers who can become peer mentors[2]
- Focus on Quick Wins: Showcase time-saving applications that deliver immediate value[24]

- Create Safe Spaces: Establish regular forums for teachers to voice concerns and share experiences[2, 3]
- Document Success: Collect and share concrete examples of how AI enhances teaching and learning[24]
- Provide Ongoing Support: Offer both formal training and informal mentoring opportunities[1, 3]

Addressing concerns head-on is crucial for building trust.[3] Teachers often worry about job security, academic integrity, and the ethical implications of AI use. These are valid concerns that deserve thoughtful discussion. Create space for open dialogue about these issues, and work together to develop clear guidelines for ethical AI use in your school.

Professional development around AI should be ongoing and differentiated, just like our instruction for students.[1, 3] Some teachers might be ready for advanced applications, while others need support with basics. That's okay; what matters is that everyone feels supported in their learning journey.

Remember that building teacher buy-in is a marathon, not a sprint. Celebrate small victories, like when a skeptical colleague successfully uses AI to create differentiated reading comprehension questions, or when a department develops new protocols for ethical AI use in student research projects.[2]

One effective approach is to establish an "AI Champions" program, where teachers who are comfortable with AI tools can mentor colleagues.[2] These champions don't need to be tech experts; they just need to be willing to learn, share, and support others. Their role is to bridge the gap between possibility and practice, showing how AI can enhance rather than replace good teaching.

As you work to build your school's AI learning community, keep these key principles in mind:

- Prioritize teacher agency in AI adoption decisions[1, 2]
- Invest in ongoing, ethical professional learning[2, 3]
- Leverage peer leadership and collaborative communities[2, 24]
- Develop transparent, inclusive policies[3]

Remember, the goal isn't to create a school full of AI experts; it's to build a community where teachers feel empowered to explore, experiment, and evolve their practice with AI as a supportive tool. When teachers feel supported in their AI journey, they're more likely to create innovative, engaging learning experiences for their students.

As you move forward in building your school's AI learning community, remember that every small step matters. Whether it's helping a colleague troubleshoot their first AI writing prompt or sharing a successful lesson plan, you're contributing to a culture of innovation that will benefit both teachers and students for years to come.

Strategic Implementation: From Pilot Programs to School-Wide Integration

Moving from small AI experiments to school-wide implementation can feel like trying to steer a massive ship with a tiny rudder; it takes careful planning, patience, and a clear sense of direction. But with the right approach, we can navigate this transition successfully while keeping our educational values firmly at the helm.

Let's start with a fundamental truth: successful AI implementation isn't about rushing to adopt every new tool. It's about thoughtful progression that prioritizes both educational effectiveness and student well-being.[62, 64, 11] The research shows that schools that take a measured, strategic approach to AI integration see better outcomes than those that rush to implement without proper planning.

Here's what a strategic implementation journey typically looks like:

- Start with a Clear Foundation: Ensure teachers have basic AI literacy and understanding of fundamental principles[62]
- Build Stakeholder Trust: Maintain open communication with families, students, and staff about AI use[64]
- Begin with Focused Pilots: Test specific AI tools in controlled settings before scaling up[62, 11]
- Measure and Adjust: Use data and feedback to refine your approach[62, 11]

One of the most effective frameworks for implementation is what researchers call the 4Cs approach to ethical AI use: Critical Thinking, Creativity, Collaboration, and Communication[64]. This framework helps ensure we're not just adding technology for technology's sake, but truly enhancing learning and teaching.

When it comes to piloting AI tools, start small but think big. Choose one department or grade level to test a specific AI application; perhaps an AI writing assistant for English classes or a feedback tool for research papers.[63, 11] Set clear objectives and assessment criteria so you can measure what's working and what needs adjustment.[62]

Here's a practical checklist for moving from pilot to full implementation:

- Develop clear AI use policies that protect student privacy and promote ethical use[64]
- Create structured professional development pathways for teachers at all comfort levels[63, 65]
- Establish regular feedback cycles to gather insights from teachers and students[64]
- Ensure equitable access to AI tools and resources across classrooms[62, 11]
- Build in time for teacher collaboration and sharing of best practices[64, 65]

One crucial aspect often overlooked is infrastructure readiness. Before scaling up, ensure your school has adequate technological infrastructure and support systems in place.[62] This includes reliable internet connectivity, device access, and technical support for both teachers and students.

Professional development is another critical piece of the puzzle. Research shows that personalized, ongoing training, including peer coaching and workshops, is more effective than one-size-fits-all approaches.[63, 65] Consider establishing an 'AI Champions' program where tech-comfortable teachers can mentor colleagues in a supportive, low-pressure environment.

As you scale up implementation, maintain focus on these key principles:

- Keep student learning at the center of all decisions
- Prioritize teacher agency and professional judgment
- Maintain transparent communication with all stakeholders[64]
- Regular evaluation and adjustment of practices[62, 11]
- Ongoing attention to ethical considerations and data privacy[64, 11]

Remember that challenges are normal and expected. Common hurdles include data privacy concerns, varying levels of teacher buy-in, and technological equity issues.[62, 11] Address these proactively by establishing clear protocols, providing robust support systems, and ensuring equitable access to resources.

One effective strategy is to assign rotating roles to students during the implementation process; such as Prompt Engineer, Bias Checker, and Fact Verifier.[64] This not only helps with digital citizenship development but also gives students agency in how AI is used in their learning.

As you move forward with implementation, keep documentation of what works and what doesn't.[62, 11] This evidence will be invaluable for refining your approach and sharing success stories with other schools. Remember, the goal isn't perfect implementation; it's thoughtful integration that enhances teaching and learning while maintaining academic integrity.

Finally, celebrate the small wins along the way. When a department successfully integrates an AI tool, when students show improved engagement, or when teachers report time savings; these are all victories worth recognizing. They help build momentum and maintain enthusiasm for continued growth and innovation.

Remember, you don't have to figure this all out alone. Many schools are on this journey, and we can learn from each other's experiences. The key is to move forward deliberately, always keeping our educational values and student needs at the forefront of our decisions.

Measuring Impact: Documenting and Sharing AI Success Stories

Let's be honest; measuring the impact of AI in our classrooms isn't just about collecting data and creating spreadsheets. It's about telling the story of how these tools are transforming teaching and learning in meaningful ways. When we document and share our AI success stories effectively, we not only validate our own practices but also inspire and guide other educators on their AI journey.

The key to measuring AI's impact starts with defining clear, measurable goals.[67, 21] What exactly are we hoping to achieve? Maybe it's reducing grading time, improving student engagement, or enhancing the quality of feedback. Whatever your objectives, they should align with your broader educational goals and be something you can actually track.

Here are some practical metrics you can use to measure AI's impact in your classroom:

- Time saved on administrative tasks and grading[21]
- Frequency and quality of student feedback[66, 21]

- Student academic performance and growth measures[67, 68]
- Student and teacher satisfaction levels
- Equity indicators (like reduction in achievement gaps)

But numbers only tell part of the story. The most compelling evidence often comes from combining quantitative data with qualitative insights. For example, when tracking the implementation of an AI writing assistant, you might collect both assessment scores and student testimonials about their writing process.

One particularly effective approach is to use what assessment experts call the "Three-Layer Documentation Method." First, gather the hard data; things like time savings, assessment scores, and usage statistics.[21] Second, collect qualitative feedback through surveys, interviews, or focus groups. Finally, create detailed case studies that show how specific AI tools addressed real classroom challenges.

When it comes to sharing your success stories, remember that transparency is crucial.[68] Be honest about both the wins and the challenges. Your colleagues will appreciate your candor, and it helps build trust in AI implementation. Always ensure you're following proper data protection guidelines and maintaining student privacy when sharing results.

Here's a framework for structuring your AI success stories:

- Start with the challenge or problem you were trying to solve
- Describe the AI solution and implementation process
- Share specific, measurable outcomes
- Include teacher and student perspectives

- Discuss lessons learned and next steps

Remember to leverage multiple channels for sharing your findings.[67, 68] This might include internal reports, professional learning communities, conferences, or even social media (with appropriate permissions, of course). The goal is to create a ripple effect of positive change across your school community.

One powerful way to document impact is through regular "AI Impact Check-ins." Set aside time each quarter to review your data, gather feedback, and reflect on progress. This not only helps track long-term trends but also identifies areas where adjustments might be needed.

When sharing your findings, use visualization tools to make your data more accessible and compelling.[69] A simple chart showing the reduction in grading time or improvement in student engagement can be worth a thousand words. Just remember to keep your presentations clear and focused on the metrics that matter most to your audience.

It's also important to consider ethical documentation practices. Monitor for algorithmic bias, ensure equitable access to AI tools, and be transparent about how AI is being used in your classroom.[68] This builds trust with students, parents, and colleagues while promoting responsible AI adoption.

Finally, don't forget to celebrate the small wins along the way. Did an AI tool help you provide more detailed feedback to students?[66] Did it free up time for more one-on-one instruction? These incremental improvements add up to significant transformations over time.

Remember, measuring and sharing AI impact isn't just about proving the technology works; it's about building a community of practice where educators can learn from each other's experiences. By documenting and sharing our successes (and yes, our challenges too), we create a roadmap for others to follow while continually improving our own practice.

As you begin documenting your AI journey, start small but think big. Choose one or two key metrics to track, gather regular feedback from students and colleagues, and share your findings in ways that resonate with your school community. You're not just measuring impact; you're helping to shape the future of education. As we wrap up our exploration of becoming an AI champion in your school, let's take a moment to reflect on the journey ahead. Leading an AI transformation isn't about being the most tech-savvy teacher in the building; it's about being a bridge builder, a storyteller, and most importantly, a supportive colleague who helps others see the possibilities in this new frontier of education.

Through Skye's story and our discussion of building teacher buy-in, implementing strategic pilots, and measuring impact, we've seen how one educator's willingness to experiment and share can ripple out to transform an entire school community. Remember, you don't need to have all the answers to be an effective AI leader. You just need to be willing to ask good questions, listen with empathy, and create spaces where your colleagues feel safe to explore and grow.

As you step into your role as an AI champion, keep these core principles in mind:

- Start small but dream big: Begin with manageable pilots that can scale
- Lead with empathy: Remember that change is challenging for everyone
- Focus on solutions: Show how AI addresses real classroom pain points
- Document and share: Let success stories inspire others
- Stay learner-centered: Keep student needs at the heart of innovation

Your journey as an AI champion will have its challenges. There will be technical hiccups, skeptical colleagues, and moments of doubt. But remember why we're doing this: to create more engaging, effective, and equitable learning experiences for our students while making teaching more sustainable for educators.

When I think back to my own early days of AI integration, I remember feeling overwhelmed by the possibilities and responsibilities. But with each small success, a time-saving workflow here, an engaged student there, I gained confidence. More importantly, I discovered that leadership isn't about having all the answers; it's about creating conditions where innovation can flourish.

As you close this book and begin your own journey as an AI champion, remember that you're not alone. There's a growing community of educators who are reimagining what's possible with AI in education. Your experiences, insights, and even your struggles will contribute to this collective wisdom.

You have everything you need to get started: a foundation of knowledge about AI tools and strategies, practical frameworks for implementation, and most importantly, your own expertise as an educator. Trust your instincts, stay curious, and keep your focus on what matters most: creating powerful learning experiences for your students.

The future of education isn't about replacing teachers with technology; it's about empowering teachers to use technology in ways that enhance their expertise and expand their impact. As an AI champion in your school, you'll help shape that future, one classroom at a time.

So take that first step. Start small, celebrate progress, and remember that every expert was once a beginner. The journey of AI integration isn't a sprint to the finish line; it's an ongoing exploration of what's possible when we combine the best of human wisdom with the power of artificial intelligence.

You've got this. And your students and colleagues will be better for having you as their guide in this exciting new chapter of education.

Conclusion

As we conclude our exploration of AI in education, let's take a moment to organize the essential tools and strategies we've discovered for leading successful AI integration in our schools. I've created what I call the "Implementation Readiness Toolkit," a practical collection of resources that will help you confidently guide your school's AI transformation.

First, let's acknowledge that change management in education requires both vision and practical support. Throughout this book, we've moved from understanding AI's potential to actively implementing it in our classrooms. Now, you're ready to take the next step: becoming a catalyst for positive change in your school community.

Your toolkit for leading this transformation includes clear communication templates, professional development frameworks, and step-by-step implementation guides. Remember to start with small wins; perhaps sharing how AI helped you reduce grading time or create more engaging lesson plans. These concrete examples will resonate with colleagues more than abstract possibilities.

I've learned that successful AI integration often follows a "ripple effect" pattern. It begins with one teacher's success story, spreads through department meetings and informal conversations, and eventually transforms entire school cultures. Your role as an innovation champion isn't to force change but to facilitate discovery and support growth.

As you move forward, keep these essential elements in mind:

- Start with willing early adopters who can help build momentum
- Document and share success stories from your school community

- Create safe spaces for experimentation and learning
- Develop clear protocols for ethical AI use
- Maintain open dialogue with all stakeholders

Remember that resistance often comes from valid concerns about student learning and academic integrity. Address these concerns head-on with evidence-based practices and clear guidelines. Share the frameworks we've explored for maintaining academic integrity while leveraging AI's benefits.

Your journey as an AI innovation champion won't always be smooth, but you now have the tools, strategies, and understanding to navigate challenges effectively. Focus on building sustainable practices that enhance rather than overwhelm your school's existing systems.

Perhaps most importantly, remember that this transformation isn't about replacing traditional teaching wisdom; it's about amplifying it. The future of education lies in finding the perfect balance between human connection and technological innovation. You're not just implementing new tools; you're helping shape how the next generation will learn, think, and create.

As you close this book and begin your implementation journey, know that you're part of a growing community of educators who are thoughtfully integrating AI into their schools. Your efforts to lead this transformation will help create more engaging, efficient, and equitable learning environments for all students.

The resources, templates, and frameworks we've explored are just the beginning. Use them as starting points, adapt them to your context, and share your innovations with others. Together, we're building a future where AI enhances rather than diminishes the human elements of education.

You have everything you need to begin this journey. Start small, think big, and remember that every significant transformation in education history began with educators like you; those willing to thoughtfully embrace new possibilities while holding firm to timeless educational values.

Now, take that first step. Your school community is ready for the AI transformation, and you're ready to lead it.

References

[1] Watson, C. E. (2024). *Teaching with AI: A Practical Guide to a New Era of Human Learning*. SoBrief.
https://sobrief.com/books/teaching-with-ai

[2] Blackwelder, A., & Cowley, J. (2025, January 17). *Future-Ready Teaching With AI: Unlocking Student Potential in the Age of Artificial Intelligence*. Corwin.
https://www.corwin.com/books/future-ready-teaching-with-ai-289524

[3] Bowen J. A. & Watson C. E. (2024, April 30). *Teaching with AI: A Practical Guide to a New Era of Human Learning*. Johns Hopkins University Press.
https://www.press.jhu.edu/books/title/53869/teaching-ai

[4] Buyserie, B. & Thurston, T. N. (2024). *Teaching and Generative AI: Pedagogical Possibilities and Productive Tensions*. Utah State University.
https://www.usu.edu/empowerteaching/publications/books/teaching-ai/

[5] Mulalic, D. (2024, December 28). *The AI Teacher's Companion: Integrating Artificial Intelligence in Your Classroom*. Barnes & Noble. https://www.barnesandnoble.com/w/the-ai-teachers-companion-davor-mulalic/1146760186

[6] Sanako. (2024, May). *What to know about AI tools for language teachers in 2025?*. Sanako. https://sanako.com/what-are-the-best-ai-tools-for-language-teachers-in-2025

[7] Harris, M. (2025, January 3). *Top Tech Tools for Teachers in 2025*. Teaching Channel. https://www.teachingchannel.com/k12-hub/blog/top-tech-tools-for-teachers-in-2025/

[8] Mohr, C. (2025, June 30). *Gemini in Classroom: No-cost AI tools that amplify teaching and learning*. Google Blog. https://blog.google/outreach-initiatives/education/classroom-ai-features/

[9] Hughes, M. (2025, May 25). *The 20 Best AI Tools for Teachers (2025)*. Chalkie. https://chalkie.ai/us/our-blog/20-best-ai-tools-for-teachers

[10] Novak, K. (2025, January 14). *Why Embracing AI is the Ultimate Power Move in Education*. Novak Education. https://www.novakeducation.com/blog/why-embracing-ai-is-the-ultimate-power-move-in-education

[11] Poth, R. D. (2023, August). *7 AI Tools That Help Teachers Work More Efficiently*. Edutopia. https://www.edutopia.org/article/7-ai-tools-that-help-teachers-work-more-efficiently/

[12] Hopkins J. M. (2024, March 7). *16 AI Tools for Education Content Creation*. Intellum. https://www.intellum.com/resources/blog/16-ai-tools-for-education-content-creation

[13] Google and MIT RAISE. (2024, January 01). *Generative AI for Educators*. Grow with Google. https://grow.google/ai-for-educators/

[14] Google. (2024). *Advancing education with AI*. Google for Education. https://edu.google.com/intl/ALL_us/ai/education/

[15] Khan, S., Fisher, D., Frey, N., Marshall, J., & Hargrave, M. (2025, July 11). *Teaching Students to Use AI Ethically & Responsibly: Exploring AI With Intentionality, Curiosity, and Care*. Corwin. https://www.corwin.com/books/teaching-students-to-use-ai-299071

[16] Magna Publications. (2023, August). *How Can I Use AI as a Student Writing and Editing Coach?*. Magna Publications. https://www.magnapubs.com/product/program/how-can-i-use-ai-as-a-student-writing-and-editing-coach/

[17] Jensen, M. (2024, March 1). *USU Creates Canvas-Integrated AI Writing Coach*. Utah State University Today. https://www.usu.edu/today/story/usu-creates-canvas-integrated-ai-writing-coach

[18] Ramos, D. C. (2025, February 5). *Faculty to Test AI Writing Coach's Ability to Advance Academic Writing and Digital Literacy in Higher Education*. CSUF News. https://news.fullerton.edu/2025/02/faculty-to-test-ai-writing-coachs-ability-to-advance-academic-writing-and-digital-literacy-in-higher-education/

[19] Florent, J. & Todd, J. (2025, February 19). *Rethinking Assessment Strategies in the Age of AI*. CAT Base. https://catwiki.xula.edu/RethinkingAssessmentStrategiesintheAgeof_AI

[20] Muncey, N. (2025, June 13). *How AI assessment tools can transform teaching and learning*. SchoolAI. https://schoolai.com/blog/ai-assessment-tools-for-educators-key-learning-insights

21 Digital Futures Institute. (2023). *Thinking about Assessment in the Time of Generative Artificial Intelligence*. Teachers College, Columbia University. https://www.tc.columbia.edu/digitalfuturesinstitute/ai-in-education/thinking-about-assessment-in-the-time-of-generative-artificial-intelligence/

22 Meakin L. A. (2024, May 13). *AI and assessment: Rethinking assessment strategies and supporting students in appropriate use of AI*. Impact Journal. https://my.chartered.college/impact_article/ai-and-assessment-rethinking-assessment-strategies-and-supporting-students-in-appropriate-use-of-ai/

23 ModernMind Publications. (2023). *Teaching With AI Summary*. Shortform. https://www.shortform.com/summary/teaching-with-ai-summary-modernmind-publications

24 Digital Commons. (2023, December 14). *Access Denied - WAF Rule Reached*. Embry-Riddle Aeronautical University Digital Commons. https://commons.erau.edu/cgi/viewcontent.cgi?article=2424&context=publication

25 Polman J. & Boardman A. (2022, January 28). *Authenticity Brings Project-Based Learning to Life: How to Ensure It's at the Center of Instruction in Your Classroom*. International Literacy Association. https://www.literacyworldwide.org/blog/literacy-now/2022/01/29/authenticity-brings-project-based-learning-to-life-how-to-ensure-it-s-at-the-center-of-instruction-in-your-classroom

26 University of Iowa Education Blog. (2024, August 19). *Digital literacy: Preparing students for a tech-savvy future*. University of

Iowa Online Programs. https://onlineprograms.education.uiowa.edu/blog/digital-literacy-preparing-students-for-a-tech-savvy-future

27 Tucker, C. R. (2023, December 1). *My Books - Practical Strategies to Reimagine Learning*. Dr. Catlin Tucker. https://catlintucker.com/my-books/

28 Miller, M. (2023, March 01). *AI for Educators*. Ditch That Textbook. https://ditchthattextbook.com/ai-edu/

29 Gates B. (2024, May 21). *Sal Khan's Must-Read Book on AI and Education*. Gates Notes. https://www.gatesnotes.com/books/education/reader/bravenewwords

30 Writers of UoPeople. (2024, November 28). *Back To Basics: What Is Performance-Based Assessment (PBA)?*. University of the People. https://www.uopeople.edu/blog/what-is-performance-based-assessment-pba/

31 Operations, Curriculum and Assessment. (2022, June 01). *Performance-Based Learning*. Schoolcraft College. https://www.schoolcraft.edu/oca/performance-based-learning/

32 Feder, H. (2023, October 19). *Performance Assessment for Parents and Policy Makers*. FairTest. https://fairtest.org/performance-assessments-for-parents-and-policy-makers/

33 Hilliard, P. (2016). *Performance-Based Assessment: Reviewing the Basics*. Edutopia. https://www.edutopia.org/blog/performance-based-assessment-reviewing-basics-patricia-hilliard

34 Awadallah Alkouk W. and Khlaif Z. N.. (2024, December 03). *AI-resistant assessments in higher education: practical insights from faculty training workshops*. Frontiers in Education. https://www.frontiersin.org/journals/education/articles/10.3389/feduc.2024.1499495/full

35 Center for Teaching and Learning. (2024, January 01). *Creating AI-Resistant Assignments, Activities, and Assessments (Designing Out)*. Northern Michigan University. https://nmu.edu/ctl/creating-ai-resistant-assignments-activities-and-assessments-designing-out

36 Murphy, S. (2024, September 27). *Outsmarting the Bots: 5 Strategies to Create AI-Resistant Assignments*. Teaching Channel. https://www.teachingchannel.com/k12-hub/blog/outsmarting-the-bots-5-strategies-to-create-ai-resistant-assignments/

37 Monsha. (2025, April 24). *30 Ideas for Generating AI-Resilient Assessments*. Monsha.ai. https://monsha.ai/blog/30-ideas-for-generating-ai-resilient-assessments

38 Mazur, E. (2025, March 20). *The Future of Assessment: Rethinking AI's Role in Teaching and Learning*. Perusall. https://www.perusall.com/blog/future-of-assessment-rethinking-ai-role-in-teaching-and-learning

39 Joyner, D. A. (2024, May 27). *A Teacher's Guide to Conversational AI: Enhancing Assessment, Instruction, and Curriculum with*

Chatbots. Routledge. https://www.routledge.com/A-Teachers-Guide-to-Conversational-AI-Enhancing-Assessment-Instruction-and-Curriculum-with-Chatbots/Joyner/p/book/9781032671154

[40] Abdous, M. (2025, January 13). *Monday Meet Ups and Teaching with AI*. Old Dominion University. https://www.odu.edu/facultydevelopment/article/monday-meet-ups-and-teaching-ai

[41] The Institute for Ethical AI in Education. (2021, March). *The Ethical Framework for AI in Education*. AI in Education. https://www.ai-in-education.co.uk/resources/the-institute-for-ethical-ai-in-education-the-ethical-framework-for-ai-in-education

[42] Georgieva M., Webb J., Stuart J., Bell J., Crawford S., and Ritter-Guth B. (2025, June 24). *AI Ethical Guidelines*. EDUCAUSE Library. https://library.educause.edu/resources/2025/6/ai-ethical-guidelines

[43] Nguyen A., Ngo H. N., Hong Y., Dang B., & Nguyen B. T. (2022, October 13). *Ethical principles for artificial intelligence in education*. Education and Information Technologies. https://link.springer.com/article/10.1007/s10639-022-11316-w

[44] The Institute for Ethical AI in Education. (2021). *The Ethical Framework for AI in Education*. OECD Events. https://www.oecd-events.org/smart-data-and-digital-technology-in-education/session/0e517bba-c801-ed11-b47a-a04a5e7cf9da/the-ethical-framework-for-ai-in-education

[45] Mekdeci, K. (2025, July 16). *Ethical Framework for Teacher Use of Generative AI*. TIE Online.

https://www.tieonline.com/article/7728/ethical-framework-for-teacher-use-of-generative-ai

46 Southern Methodist University. (2025, January 19). *How to use AI in the classroom ethically and responsibly*. SMU Online Learning Sciences Blog. https://learningsciences.smu.edu/blog/how-to-use-ai-in-the-classroom

47 DerSimonian, R. & Montagnino, C. (2025, June 18). *Crafting Thoughtful AI Policy in Higher Education: A Guide for Institutional Leaders*. Faculty Focus. https://www.facultyfocus.com/articles/academic-leadership/crafting-thoughtful-ai-policy-in-higher-education-a-guide-for-institutional-leaders/

48 Bowen, J. A. & Watson, C. E. (2025, December 2). *Teaching with AI: A Practical Guide to a New Era of Human Learning*. Johns Hopkins University Press. https://www.press.jhu.edu/books/title/54122/teaching-ai

49 Digital Learning Institute. (2023, August 15). *Exploring AI in eLearning Content Creation*. Digital Learning Institute. https://www.digitallearninginstitute.com/blog/exploring-ai-in-elearning-content-creation

50 Khan, J. (2024, April 17). *Leveraging AI for Next-Gen Education: Crafting Adaptive Content*. Quixl. https://www.quixl.ai/blog/leveraging-ai-in-education-crafting-adaptive-content-for-next-generation/

[51] Pulido, L. (2024, April). *6 AI Use Cases in Educational Content Creation*. Ease Learning. https://easelearning.com/all-posts/6-ai-use-cases-in-educational-content-creation/

[52] Shah, K. (2024, July 29). *Leveraging AI for Next-Gen Education: Crafting Adaptive Content*. Third Rock Techkno. https://www.thirdrocktechkno.com/blog/leveraging-ai-for-next-gen-education-crafting-adaptive-content/

[53] Fora Soft. (2025, July 5). *The Ultimate Guide To AI-Assisted Educational Content Creation*. Fora Soft Blog. https://www.forasoft.com/blog/article/ai-assisted-educational-content-creation

[54] Ausbert. (2025, February 24). *Best Differentiation Strategies Assisted by the Top 3 AI Tools for Teachers in 2025*. Edcafe. https://www.edcafe.ai/blog/ai-assisted-differentiation-strategies

[55] Muncey, N. (2025, June 11). *Strategies for enhancing differentiated instruction using AI tutors*. SchoolAI. https://schoolai.com/blog/strategies-using-ai-tutors-improve-differentiated-instruction

[56] AI for Education. (2023, December 14). *Using AI for Differentiated Instruction*. AI for Education. https://www.aiforeducation.io/using-ai-for-differentiated-instruction

[57] Guhlin, M. (2025, February 25). *Differentiated Learning Powered by AI*. TCEA Blog. https://blog.tcea.org/differentiated-learning-powered-by-ai/

58 R3 Collaboratives. (2025, January 01). *Amplify Coaching, Transform Instruction*. Edthena. https://www.edthena.com/ai-coach-for-teachers/

59 Taylor, C. (2025, July 15). *Using the 4Cs to build an ethical AI implementation plan for schools*. SchoolAI. https://schoolai.com/blog/using-4cs-build-ethical-ai-implementation-plan-schools

60 Watson J. M. (2024, November 26). *Learning with AI: The K-12 Teacher's Guide to a New Era of Human Learning*. Johns Hopkins University Press. https://www.press.jhu.edu/books/title/54027/learning-ai

61 Digital Commons. (2023, December 12). *Access Denied - WAF Rule Reached*. CE-JEME. https://www.ce-jeme.org/cgi/viewcontent.cgi?article=1090&context=journal

62 Owan, V. J. (2023, August 01). *Exploring the potential of artificial intelligence tools in educational measurement and assessment*. Eurasia Journal of Mathematics, Science and Technology Education. https://www.ejmste.com/article/exploring-the-potential-of-artificial-intelligence-tools-in-educational-measurement-and-assessment-13428

63 Bulut, O., Beiting-Parrish, M., Casabianca, J. M., Slater, S. C., Jiao, H., Song, D., Ormerod, C. M., Fabiyi, D. G., Ivan, R., Walsh, C., Rios, O., Wilson, J., Yildirim-Erbasli, S. N., Wongvorachan, T., Liu, J. X., Tan, B., & Morilova, P. (2024, June 27). *The Rise of Artificial*

Intelligence in Educational Measurement: Opportunities and Ethical Challenges. arXiv. https://arxiv.org/abs/2406.18900

[64] Sliwinski, D. (2025, May 20). *How to Measure the Impact of Education with AI: A Step-by-Step Guide.* Intellum. https://www.intellum.com/resources/blog/measure-impact-with-ai

Thank You for Reading!

I hope you found *The AI-Powered Classroom A Teacher's Step-by-Step Guide to Using AI in Education* helpful and enjoyable!
Your feedback is invaluable to me and helps others discover this book.

If you could take a moment to **leave a review**, I'd greatly appreciate it.   Scan the QR code below to leave your review:

Thank you,

Patty R. Adams